Real life, real answers.

How to borrow money and use credit

Real life, real answers.

How to borrow money and use credit

by
Martin Weiss

Houghton Mifflin Company   Boston
1990

For information about permission to reproduce selections from this book, write to
Permissions, Houghton Mifflin Company, 2 Park Street, Boston, Massachusetts
02108.

Library of Congress Catalog Card Number: 89-85917
ISBN: 0-395-51092-9

General editors: Barbara Binswanger, James Charlton, Lee Simmons

Design by Hudson Studio

"Real life, real answers" is a trademark of the John Hancock Mutual Life Insurance
Company.

Printed in the United States of America

10 9 8 7 6 5 4 3 2 1

Although this book is designed to provide accurate and authoritative information in
regard to the subject matter covered, neither the author and general editors nor the
publisher are engaged in rendering legal, accounting, or other professional service.
If legal advice or other expert assistance is required, the services of a competent
professional should be sought.

Contents

Introduction

The days of being able to pay cash for every purchase have long since passed. Today's modern economy requires practically everyone to borrow and use credit. Properly controlled and limited, buying on credit can make your life easier, more enjoyable, and more comfortable.

Unfortunately, many people don't know enough about the credit and borrowing process, so they overborrow, pay too much in interest, and put their financial futures in great jeopardy. Every year, increasing numbers of people from all walks of life get themselves into serious debt problems. Disregarding basic principles regarding when, how, and where to borrow can wipe out years of hard work and savings.

A personal credit rating is both precious and fragile, subject to loss or impairment for any number of reasons—justified and unjustified. You cannot rely upon the statements, promises, and advertisements of banks, credit card companies, or merchants. While there are federal, state, and local laws that offer you some protection from the more scurrilous and underhanded tactics of creditors, getting into trouble over credit is still a nasty business.

This book will give you a basic understanding of many of the problems, pitfalls, and procedures surrounding the complex process of getting, keeping, and losing credit. It will help you know what to look for in a loan and what to look out for in virtually any transaction involving credit. It will also help if you are already in trouble. But it is no substitute for professional advice. If you do not understand a problem or are unable to resolve a credit matter to your satisfaction, do not hesitate to get competent legal help as soon as possible.

CHAPTER I

Credit, the double-edged sword

B uying on credit is a double-edged sword, not a magic wand. Properly handled, credit can enable you and your family to enjoy comforts and conveniences before you have accumulated enough savings to pay cash. However, misuse or overuse credit, and your life (and that of your family) can become a nightmare of incredible worry and tension. The pressure to keep up with the Joneses, the many opportunities to use credit, and the ease with which credit can be obtained, combine to tempt most of us, at one time or another, to incur debt obligations beyond our ability to repay. If you then throw in the not-so-unusual crises of temporary unemployment, a sudden medical emergency, or a burned-out automobile transmission, you have the recipe for a family about to be trapped in the vicious circle of severe financial distress.

NOT ME!

Strange as it may seem, many people who whip out the plastic card to charge a few items don't think of themselves as borrowing money and adding to their future financial burdens. That little bit of plastic seems like an easy and perfect ticket to instant gratification and happiness. Make no mistake about it; whether you charge that vacation weekend for two on your American Express card; step into your friendly neighborhood bank and sign up for that $5,000 home improvement loan; or buy shares on that hot stock tip your brother-in-law gave you by using a margin account, you are borrowing money from someone who expects to be paid back.

Besides death and taxes, there are two more things you can be sure of. No one can predict the future with absolute certainty, and all lenders want to be repaid on time and in full! This means that borrowing money and buying on credit entails taking a calculated risk. How big that risk is and whether or not you should take it depends upon your answers to two simple, but very important, questions:

1. Do my reasons for borrowing money now make good sense?
2. Do I have an intelligent and realistic plan for paying back the money I will have borrowed?

If your answer to either of these questions is "no" or "maybe," then you had better postpone taking the risk until you can honestly answer "yes" to both.

TWO KINDS OF COST

Remember, going into debt always exacts a financial cost and quite frequently an emotional cost as well. You will pay interest (and perhaps additional fees) for the privilege of making a purchase now before you are able to pay cash. You will be giving someone else extra money of yours because you would not or could not wait. If that $1,200 giant refrigerator-freezer is bought on a 12-month installment plan at 18 percent interest, typically you will make payments of $110 per month for a total cost of $1,320—$120 extra for the convenience of having that appliance now.

Beyond the dollar costs, there are also emotional costs you must be concerned with. Knowing that you owe money—that next month and for many months afterward you must make regular payments to repay the debt and interest out of your paycheck—can make anyone anxious and nervous. All too often, enjoyment of the items purchased quickly turns to regret when it becomes necessary to stretch your paycheck to cover both debt payments and your normal, day-to-day living expenses. This is especially true when the debt payments last months or even years longer than the item for which you first borrowed the money.

WHY BORROW NOW?

Going into debt, either by buying on credit or by taking out a direct loan, is as American as apple pie. Almost everyone you know owes money to somebody for the mortgage on a house, the automobile purchased on an installment contract, credit cards, charge accounts, personal loans, education loans, margin accounts, etc. Few of us have the financial capacity to buy everything we need or want in cash. Most of us can't plunk down $10,000 to $12,000 in hard cash to buy a standard Ford or Chevy sedan. Practically no one can ante up the $75,000 to $125,000 for the typical three-bedroom house. Using credit for such purposes is a perfectly normal thing to do. Using it wisely is less common.

There are a number of sound reasons for going into debt, provided the amount of debt, the interest to be charged on that debt, and the rate of repayment are all within your financial and emotional capacity. The most common are:

1. To purchase necessary big-ticket items (house, car, major appliances, etc.).
2. To purchase certain items you really need or could use now that are being offered at an exceptionally low price. Similarly, if you will definitely need an item in the near future but expect it to rise sharply in price, buying on credit now may make sense.
3. To pay for college or other educational needs. You are, after all, borrowing for something that should pay for itself in terms of creating extra future earning capacity. Given the escalating costs of education today, many families have no choice but to go into debt.
4. To deal with true emergency situations. Sudden, unanticipated

events can disrupt the financial stability of any household, often quite beyond what the immediate cash or available savings levels can handle. The definition of a "true emergency," however, requires strict interpretation and self-control.

5. To fund a new household or family. The judicious use of credit is appropriate when forming a new household, provided you have sound reasons for each credit purchase and a realistic plan for repayment. But it is a dangerous period for many. Being young is wonderful; being young and heavily in debt is terrible.

WHEN NOT TO BORROW

Just as there are perfectly sound reasons to borrow, there are fundamental reasons why borrowing should be avoided. In fact, the first step in learning how to use credit wisely is learning when not to use it, and being honest in assessing your reasons for borrowing money.

1. Impulse buying and using credit for the purchase is a double blow to financial security. Often, those impulse items are offered with easy, long-payout credit terms that make them too irresistible to pass up.

2. Trying to keep up with the Joneses is another credit no-no. You may be envious when your neighbor has an interior decorator install new wall-to-wall carpeting, but he may be able to afford it; you cannot.

3. For some people, a shopping trip is a way to cheer themselves up, and it seems so easy with a credit card. But a shopping spree may result in a real case of depression when the monthly credit card statement comes in.

4. If you are already borrowing to make ends meet, or you owe so much that you are at the limit of your ability to repay, you should not incur more debt unless it is part of a logical debt consolidation plan. Adding to an already barely manageable debt load is inviting disaster.

5. Borrowing in the vague expectation that you will be getting a raise or some other income booster to pay off the debt is a dangerous tactic. Far better to wait until the additional income

is assured before it is counted on for debt repayment.

6. Borrowing to speculate on risky ventures is not a smart use of your credit capacity. If, however, you have made a complete and thorough investigation of an investment with a reasonable amount of potential, using debt may be an intelligent way to take advantage of the opportunity. Because it may take some time before the investment is able to generate income, you must consider the drain on your current income for interest and/or principal payments on that debt during the interim. Above all, beware of the "get rich quick" scheme. The old adage still makes sense: "If it sounds too good to be true, it probably is."

OILING THE WHEELS OF COMMERCE

Granting you credit—that is, letting you borrow—is an element of marketing for the sellers of products and lenders of money. They *want* you to buy and actively encourage you to go into debt. If everyone had to pay cash for purchases, our consumer-driven economy would grind to a shuddering halt. Your own wants and desires, the enticing advertisements ("No money down and no payments for the first three months."), the preapproved credit cards sent to you in the mail ("Instant credit! Just fill out the enclosed form and return it to us.")—all combine to put you under constant pressure to go into debt.

Intelligent management of your finances requires discipline, knowledge, and planning. There is nothing tricky about it. You can do it if you make an honest effort and get the cooperation of the other members of your family.

CHAPTER II

Credit strength

T he most fundamental step in considering the use of credit is arriving at a complete understanding of how much credit your income level will permit you to handle comfortably. This is something you *cannot* leave to the lenders to determine. Remember, all the sellers of products and grantors of credit care about is getting you to buy. They won't worry and have sleepless nights because you are struggling to pay your bills. They know that, somehow, most people do manage to pay their bills and debts, often only after considerable personal anguish and family hardship. The decisions about when, how much, and under what terms you will make use of credit are your responsibility.

Your credit strength—that is, your borrowing power and the ability to pay debts back—is an enormous asset that needs careful management. There are two very distinct but closely related components to credit strength.

Repayment ability

Given your present income and the existing demands on that income for your normal living expenses and other debt repayments, there will be a finite limit to how much new or additional debt you will be able to reliably repay over a given period of time. Many lenders are quite willing to overestimate your ability to repay, with the result being that you end up with more borrowing power than you, under normal circumstances, should use. Yes, there are guidelines and "rules of thumb" regarding how much a person should borrow, but they cannot and do not apply in every individual case. It is always best to be conservative.

Borrowing power

How much credit-granting organizations are willing to lend you is based on a variety of their own measures, including your earning power, job, existing debts, past history, interest rate to be charged, etc. It is important to note that a lender's measurement of your personal borrowing power may be quite different from your own.

MEASURING CREDIT STRENGTH

Before you plunge into the treacherous waters of credit and borrowing, you must first take an honest, conservative measure of your financial position. Whether you are now or intend to be a borrower in the future, the beginning of any attempt to manage your money is the creation of a family budget and spending plan.

If you do not presently have a budget, then you must create an accurate picture of your family's income and expenditure pattern, using information readily available to you. You (and your spouse) should gather up the checkbook and bank statements, paycheck stubs, last year's tax return, paid and unpaid bills and receipts, and pencil and paper. It isn't necessary to be a certified public accountant to do this; it will take only an evening or two, especially if you follow the guidelines on the following worksheet. It is important to get input from all the members of your family regarding where and how money is spent.

Since the worksheet involves looking backward in order to project your future expenditure pattern, you must make adjustments for all new or anticipated situations (new home or apartment, additional dependents, braces for a child, someone entering college, etc.) on the expected expenditure side. Do not project any income increase unless there is absolutely no question that it will occur. When in doubt, be conservative. Note that the worksheet requires you to separate your monthly expenses from those that occur quarterly, semiannually, and annually.

FINANCIAL WORKSHEET TO ARRIVE AT YOUR NET CASH FLOW POSITION

Monthly income

(In calculating monthly income, remember that not all months will consist of four weekly paychecks. Some months have four checks; others have five checks. If you get paid weekly, add up thirteen consecutive weeks' checks, then calculate the average check amount by dividing that total by 13. Multiply that average check amount by 4.33 and insert the calculated number on line 1 below.)

1. Your regular net take-home pay (exclude overtime
   or any special income items that vary considerably) $ *1390*
2. Spouse's regular net take-home pay (exclude overtime
   or any special income items that vary considerably)   _____
3. Other income, such as dividends, interest, Social Security
   benefits, etc. (be certain that any amounts included here may be
   relied upon to continue at the same or higher level in the future)   _____

4. Monthly income total (lines 1 through 3) $ *1390*

Monthly expenses

5. Rent or mortgage payment $ *350*
6. Food (household and at work)   *200*
7. Home electric/gas/oil   *50*
8. Water and sewer   *15*
9. Telephone   *10*
10. Auto insurance   _____
11. Life insurance (not paid by employer)   _____
12. Health and accident insurance (not paid by employer)   _____
13. Homeowners insurance (if not already part
    of mortgage payment)   _____
14. Transportation and auto expenses   *40*
15. Entertainment (restaurants, movies, sports, etc.)   *100*
16. Gifts and charitable contributions   _____
17. Day-care and babysitting costs   _____
18. Investments and savings set aside   _____
19. Other (cable TV, landscape, cleaning, etc.)   *10*

20. Total monthly expenses (lines 5 through 19) $ *775*

Annual expenses

(For purposes of this worksheet, annualize the amounts paid out quarterly and semiannually.)

21. Federal, state, or local income taxes (not deducted from paycheck—check last year's tax return to see if deductions were sufficient to cover all income) $ _____
22. Real estate taxes (not included in mortgage payment) _____
23. Medical and dental bills (not covered by insurance) _2ɔ0_
24. Vacation expenses _500_
25. Tuition and education costs _____
26. Clothing _200_
27. Repairs and maintenance costs and contracts _____
28. Insurance premiums (if not included in above lists) _1400_
29. Major purchases (if not included in above lists) _____
30. Support payments (alimony, child support, and parental support) _____
31. Other (organization dues, subscriptions, etc.) _____

32. Total annual expenses (lines 21 through 31) $ _2300_

33. Divide line 32 $ _2300_ by 12 = $ _190_

Total annual expenses are divided by 12 to arrive at the amount to be set aside each month to cover these annual expenses.

Payments on debts now owed (not included in above list)

34. Personal loans from	Balance owed	Monthly payment
a. _____	$ _____	$ _____
b. _____	_____	_____
c. _____	_____	_____

35. Charge accounts from	Balance owed	Monthly payment
a. Sears	$ 1204.00	$ 27.00
b. Wallach's	1450ʊ	40.00
c. BANK ONE CompuCard	1450.00	40.00

36. Credit cards from	Balance owed	Monthly payment
a. CITIBANK USA	$ 950.00	$ 30.00
b. CITI BANK MC	950.00	30.00
c. INDependence	2701.00	80.00

37. Other loans and debts	Balance owed	Monthly payment
a. FIRST CARD	$ 2009.00	$ 45.00
b. CBT.	3413.00	244.51
c. NORTHEAST SAVINGS	1500.00	66.00

38. Total monthly payments owed on current debts $ _602.51_

Add lines 34a through 37c inclusive and insert total on line 38. Monthly payments should include interest charged.

Expenditure summary

39. Total monthly expenses as shown on line 20 $ 775.00
40. One-twelfth of annual expenses as shown on line 33   190.00
41. Total monthly payments owed as shown on line 38   603.00

42. Total monthly outlay (lines 39 through line 41) $ 1568.00

Add lines 39 through 41 inclusive and insert the amount at line 42 to arrive at what your average monthly cash outlays are expected to equal. Note that this is an average, and there can be significant variations on a month-to-month basis when quarterly, semiannual, or annual payments are made.

Net cash flow position

43. Amount on line 4 (monthly income total) $ 1390
Deduct:
44. Amount on line 42 (total monthly outlay) $ 1568.00

45. Net cash flow position (line 43 minus line 44) $ (178)

If a positive number results after subtracting line 44 (your "outgo") from line 43 (your income), it means that you have that much money available to put toward additional savings or to make payments on additional debt. But a positive number is insufficient reason to run out and sign up for a loan. You must still examine your reasons. Do they pass the test outlined in Chapter I?

If the result is a negative amount, it means you are in over your head and are probably having great difficulty in meeting existing commitments. You are either well into or about to enter a financial crisis. Now is not the time to undertake new expenditures or new obligations (unless part of an intelligently structured debt consolidation and repayment plan). You should, instead, make a careful review of where and how you are spending your income with a view to reducing expenses where possible. This is easier said than done, and may cause considerable friction within any family. Unfortunately, there is no effective substitute, short of winning the lottery, for tightening up the budget and sticking to it.

NET WORTH

In addition to your income, another important component of your credit strength is called net worth. Basically, your net worth is the total of the assets you own minus the total of the liabilities you owe. At least once a year, you should take the time to recalculate your net worth. It may seem like another job for a certified public accountant, but with a little care, you can do a reasonably accurate job.

As time passes, your net worth should increase through savings, investments, and the acquisition of assets (home, furniture, pension plan vesting, etc.) and/or the reduction of liabilities (mortgage, installment loans, etc.) as debts are paid off or reduced. If, on a year-to-year basis, your net worth is not increasing, you need a serious review of your financial planning, including budgeting, savings, and investment.

Collateral—a word that makes lenders happy

Some of the specific assets that make up your net worth can serve as collateral: an asset pledged to a lender as security that the debt will be paid. For example, when a mortgage is taken out on a house, the house is pledged as collateral for that loan. If the mortgage payments are not made, the lender may, through a legal process known as foreclosure, take title and possession of the house. The lender then may sell the house, applying the proceeds of that sale toward repayment of the unpaid balance of the mortgage plus additional legal costs and charges.

Even if a specific asset is not to be pledged as security for a loan, your accumulation of a reasonable amount of net worth serves to enhance your reputation and creditworthiness to the lending organizations.

Estimating net worth

Preparing a schedule of your net worth is like taking a snapshot; it is a picture at only one specific moment in time. All the values you place on your assets are estimates of *current market value*—that is, what each item would bring you if sold today. How much the item cost when you purchased it is not necessarily what it would sell for today. Yes, some things may be worth more, but most personal property (furniture, cars, clothes, etc.) will be worth considerably less. A used, three-year-old refrigerator that was $700 when bought new at Sears or a $200 set of curtains you installed last year are not going to bring the price you paid for them.

When estimating the market value of personal property and household goods, you probably can't count on getting more than 10 to 20 cents on the dollar, and that only if the items are no more than two years old. Even collectibles such as stamps, coins, figurines, and the like won't bring the price quoted in the value guides. For some items, say stocks and bonds, estimated market value can change quickly and their value will probably be different the very next day. Real estate values also change up or down, although not quite as rapidly.

Getting information

In order to estimate the value of some of your assets, you will have to use outside sources. With a little imagination, you can find a number of different sources to give you reasonably accurate market values. Your local library has several books that give the current values of used cars. The prices of stocks, bonds, and mutual funds can be looked up in the financial section of your newspaper, or you can ask your broker for current market value. The cash value of your life insurance and any annuities you own may be determined from a table included in your policy documents, or from your agent.

The personnel department at your place of work should be able to give you the current cash value of your vested pension or profit sharing plan if you were to quit now. Your house and any other real estate you own can be valued by checking with a real estate agent or finding out what similar real estate has sold for recently. Your IRA or Keogh plan should be valued at its present balance less any penalty you would be subject to for premature withdrawal. The periodic statement from your IRA or Keogh plan custodian or broker usually provides sufficient information for you to make an accurate valuation. Although it may cost you a fee, there are appraisers with the knowledge to put accurate values on such items as furs, jewelry, and collectibles.

Valuing a business is usually a complex matter because there are many variables involved. Most owners typically place a higher value on their business than it would actually sell for on the market. In the absence of any professional appraisal of the business, and for purposes of this worksheet only, you can use the greater of either one of the following (adjusted for your percentage of ownership): the net after-tax earnings of the business multiplied by six; the net total of stockholders'/owners' equity plus 10 percent; or the total of salary and dividends you took out of the business over the most recent full year multiplied by three. Any of these three alternatives will give you a basis to work with. Once selected, stay with the same basis in future analyses unless you have obtained a different, definitive value from a credible outside source.

While preparing a summary of your net worth is not an exact science, the result is an excellent measure of financial accomplishment, progress, and potential borrowing power.

If your liabilities are greater than your assets, you have a serious financial problem. Declaring personal bankruptcy may be necessary, but you should first seek immediate guidance from your attorney. Bankruptcy is not a step to be taken lightly or hastily (see Chapter X). The reasons why your liabilities may exceed your assets are endless: overspending; bad luck; bad investments; medical emergencies; sudden unemployment; the list goes on and on. Everybody in this precarious financial condition has his or her own sad story to tell, but many cases could have been prevented with sound financial planning, management, and spending discipline.

FINANCIAL WORKSHEET TO ARRIVE AT YOUR NET WORTH

Prepared as of: _____, 19____

Assets (what you own)

Cash and cash equivalents

Cash on hand	$ _____
Checking accounts	_____
Savings accounts	_____
Money market funds	_____
Savings bonds	_____
Certificates of deposit	_____
Treasury bills	_____
Total cash and cash equivalents	$ _____

Liquid investments—items that can readily be converted to cash
(Use estimated current market value)

Stocks	$ _____
Bonds	_____
Mutual funds	_____
Government funds and securities	_____
Cash value of life insurance	_____
Other _____	_____
_____	_____
Total liquid investments	$ _____

Nonliquid investments—items that are difficult or impossible to convert into cash on short notice (Use estimated current market value)

IRA or Keogh retirement savings plans	$ _____
Vested interest in a pension or profit-sharing plan (money to which you would be entitled, even if you left the company)	
Annuities	_____
Your house or condo	_____
Other real estate investments	_____
Your business (value of your ownership share)	_____
Loans made to others	_____
Other _____	_____
Total nonliquid investments	$ _____

Personal property

Cars $ _____

Household furnishings and appliances _____

Furs and jewelry _____

Antiques, art work, collections _____

Clothing _____

Other _____ _____

Total personal property $ _____

TOTAL ASSETS $ _____

Liabilities (what you owe)

Unpaid bills

Rent or mortgage payment $ _____

Utilities _____

Taxes _____

Medical and dental bills _____

Insurance premiums _____

Alimony, child support, parental support _____

Charge account balances _____

Credit card balances _____

Other _____ _____

_____ _____

Total unpaid bills $ _____

Loans

Home mortgage (first and second) $_____

Home improvement _____

Home equity _____

Auto _____

Education _____

Personal _____

From family and friends _____

Installment _____

Life insurance _____

Margin accounts _____

Other _____ _____

_____

Total loans $ _____

TOTAL LIABILITIES $ _____

16

Summary of net worth

Total assets (from above)	$ _____
Deduct:	
Total liabilities (from above)	$ _____
NET WORTH	$ _____

If your assets exceed your liabilities, you are on your way to developing and increasing financial stability. By taking a measure of your net worth once a year at the same time each year, you will be able to judge your progress in meeting the financial goals and objectives you set for yourself and your family.

THE PICTURE OF HEALTH

From a lender's standpoint, the more substantial your net worth is, the more attractive you are as a potential borrower. While lenders look to the size and consistency of your current income stream (usually salary) as the primary source of repayment, they will also look at your net worth. Your ability to create personal net worth not only conveys the impression of reliability and responsibility, but your various assets will serve as the collection point of last resort if you are otherwise unable to repay a loan. Many lenders will require you to pledge some or all of your net worth as security for loan repayment.

HOW MUCH IS TOO MUCH?

One of the guidelines used by lending institutions in determining how much they are willing to lend is the 20/25 percent rule. Basically, the lender wants to try to keep the aggregate amount of your debt payments (including interest) to within 20 to 25 percent (excluding mortgage payments) of your annual income. If, for example, you earned $36,000 a year, the lending institution would not want to see you paying out more than $7,200 to

$9,000 per year in payments toward all your debts, including the loan you are now seeking.

Years of experience in lending money has shown that putting most individuals in a position where more than 25 percent of their income has to go for debt service (excluding mortgage payments) is inviting financial disaster; it is just too much for most people to handle, given the normal day-to-day living expenses.

If mortgage payments are included, that limit is usually raised to 36 percent, but it is structured differently. For a typical mortgage, the lender does not want to see more than 28 percent of the gross earnings going for debt service (principal, interest, real estate taxes, homeowners insurance, etc.) relating to the mortgage. Thus, allowing 28 percent for a mortgage means that not more than 8 percent of gross income should be allocated to cover other loans or debts (for example, auto loans, credit card balances, or personal loans).

Are there exceptions? Certainly, but don't count on being one, even if you have a perfect credit record. Moreover, the guidelines may not be appropriate for your individual situation. You may know some things that the guidelines haven't taken into consideration. For example, if you know that in a few months you will need to help support your aged mother, or that the expensive dental work you've been postponing will have to be done, then it would be best for you to stay at or below the low end of the guidelines.

CHAPTER III

Establishing and keeping a good credit rating

I magine yourself as the president of a big bank or lending organization with dozens of offices throughout the city, perhaps hundreds throughout the country.

WHO ARE YOU, STRANGER?

You know that every day, many people you have never seen before and don't know the first thing about—absolute strangers—will be coming into your various branches to borrow money. Statistics and history tell you that some of these strangers will be crooks trying to borrow money with no intention of ever repaying. Others will be honest folks who, for various reasons, will get in over their heads and will be unable to repay. Your employees (most of whom you also don't know very well) will be deciding whether and how much of the company's money to lend these strangers.

Remember, your company is in the business of money-lending. You *want* to lend as much money as practical, but you also want to be repaid on time and with the minimum of problems. How do you decide who will be granted a loan and who will be rejected?

More than likely, Mr. President, you will do the same thing thousands of other money-lending organizations have done.

You will make your organization follow a more or less standard credit review and approval system. Drawing upon years of experience in making both good (paid off) and bad (slow or non-collectible) loans, lending institutions have established fairly rigid criteria and procedures in order to maximize the frequency of good credit risks and minimize the frequency of bad ones. Often, the various criteria are specifically targeted or weighted for the customer base from which the lending institution wants the majority of its customers to come.

For example, the credit approval criteria for an organization that expects to draw its customers from shoppers for expensive, high-fashion clothes will probably be different from the criteria of a mass-market, discount retailer. The criteria for "platinum" or "gold" American Express cards are higher than for the standard "green" American Express card.

Before granting credit to anyone, your employees will have the person seeking credit fill out a lengthy application form that requires extensive background information of both a financial and personal nature. On the basis of that information and, most likely, a credit report supplied by a credit bureau (an organization whose primary purpose is to investigate and report on the detailed credit history of individuals), your employees will then decide if, how much, and on what terms they will lend money. That, Mr. President, is how you will run your money-lending business. And that is the system your own credit application will pass through when you attempt to obtain approval for loans and credit cards.

SCORING POINTS FOR CREDIT

Most loan or credit applications require the same basic information (see the sample form on page 21). When you fill in the blanks you are giving the creditor information that will then be correlated against "response categories" that have a certain weight or score toward qualifying for credit. If your application

APPLICANT

LAST NAME		FIRST	MIDDLE INIT

MAIL ADDRESS	COUNTY	SINCE (MO/YR)

CITY	STATE	ZIP CODE	PHONE

RENT ☐ OWN/BUY ☐ COST OF HOME   CURRENT VALUE   BAL. OWING
OTHER ☐ _____ $ $ $

PYMT/RENT   TO WHOM PAID   ADDRESS
$

FORMER ADDRESS IF LESS THAN 3 YEARS AT PRESENT	STREET	CITY	STATE

MARITAL STATUS: ☐ MARRIED
                 ☐ UNMARRIED
                 ☐ SEPARATED

SOCIAL SEC. NO.   BIRTH DATE (MO/YR) DEPENDENTS:
                                              ____ CHILDREN ____ OTHER

OCCUPATION AND INCOME

EMPLOYER   OCCUPATION

EMPL ADDRESS

DATE OF EMPL (MO/YR)   MO SALARY - GROSS   EMPL PHONE

ADDITIONAL INCOME $ NATURE
                                    INCLUSION OF ALIMONY, CHILD SUPPORT
                                    OR SEPARATE MAINTENANCE IS OPTIONAL

PREVIOUS EMPLOYER IF LESS THAN 3 YRS. WITH PRESENT   HOW LONG   ADDRESS

DEPOSIT ACCOUNTS

TYPE	COMPANY NAME & LOCATION	ACCT NUMBER	APPROX BAL
CHECKING			
SAVINGS			
☐ SAVINGS & LN ☐ CREDIT UNIONS			

INDEBTEDNESS

TYPE	COMPANY NAME & LOCATION	ACCOUNT NO	BALANCE	MO PYMTS
MORTGAGE				
SECOND MORTGAGE				
AUTO MAKE YR				
AUTO MAKE YR				
CREDIT CARD				
CREDIT CARD				
CREDIT UNION				
OTHER				

21

adds up to an acceptable score, it stands a good chance of being approved. If not, it will be rejected.

For example, in some areas of the country, creditors would prefer to grant credit to home owners rather than home renters. Therefore, your response to the question that asks whether you rent or own your home will get a higher score if you respond that you own your home. Because it indicates some level of financial planning and stability, an individual with a savings account will probably score higher than someone without such an account.

Some occupations score higher than others. Describing your job as "data entry clerk" may score lower than if your response is "computer input specialist." Being a sanitary engineer sounds considerably more creditworthy than being a janitor. You may not agree, but, the more important and responsible your job title sounds, the more points it will score. Since statistics indicate that individuals with a higher education level are better credit risks, creditors sometimes infer your level of education from your job title, even if they don't ask specific questions about your education.

Obviously, one of the key questions is your income. All other things being equal, which they rarely are, the higher the income level the more points scored, although this is not always true. On a typical credit application you will be asked about other loans or credit payments you are making. If Mr. Jones says he has $40,000 a year in take-home pay, out of which he is already committed to making large monthly payments for a mortgage, an auto loan, a home improvement loan, and a credit union loan, the credit organization might very well give a higher score to Mr. Smith, who earns $30,000 a year but is paying off only a small auto loan.

An individual with a history of taking out numerous loans from small loan companies (which are sometimes considered lenders of last resort to the desperate) is painting a picture of someone constantly in financial trouble. More than likely, that will detract from his or her creditworthiness score.

However, one of the best ways to score high is to have good relations with other creditors. If you provide credit references that, upon verification, indicate that you have paid off prior loans on time and/or been prompt in meeting your Visa, American Express, or other credit card payments, you should score quite well. The credit report on you will also indicate the status of your relations with your creditors.

How much verification?

How honest should you be on your credit application? Some minor exaggeration is probably OK, maybe even expected, but to attempt to create a whole new picture is sure to get you rejected. There are too many facts that have to be consistent with one another and there is always the reality of the credit report lurking in the background. Some, but not all, banks will call your employer to verify your level of compensation.

Will a bank try to find out if you've actually lived in your house six years? How will they know you are trying to feed, clothe, and educate six kids on your income instead of the two you put into the application? The truth is that lying is risky and can backfire. Remember, there are legal penalties for fraud.

If you have a credit problem lurking in your background, don't try to hide it. It will probably show up anyway on the report the lender will receive from the credit bureau. If you voluntarily bring the problem up and disclose it, you will have the opportunity to explain it. Maybe your ex-spouse ran up some bills on your credit card that had to be worked out. Perhaps your company went on strike for seven months in 1984 and you couldn't keep up with all the mortgage and department store payments for a while. You will make a far better impression on the loan officer if you are frank about past credit problems than if he or she finds out about them from other sources.

GETTING CREDIT

Because much of anyone's credit history is derived from computerized information regarding banking, credit card, and charge account transactions, someone who always pays cash will be "invisible" to the system. Similarly, people who have never had credit in their own name (widows, divorcees, young people just starting out on their own) will have some difficulty in getting credit approval. They have no individual credit or earnings histories that can be reviewed by the credit-granting organizations. They may have been on a job for too brief a time to create the picture of reliability and competence that the creditors are looking for. Even so, with some careful planning, you can establish your own creditworthiness, at least for a small amount, and then build it up from there as justified and needed.

You should start developing your credit and financial history early, even if you have no immediate intention of borrowing money. Waiting until after you need credit instead of establishing it beforehand just doesn't make good sense. Many things can go wrong during the credit approval process that might leave you high and dry in an emergency situation. Start working on establishment of credit as soon as you can. If you run into problems, you will know what they are and possibly have sufficient time to correct them.

CHECKING ACCOUNTS

Find a neighborhood bank that is convenient and has a reputation for friendliness and courtesy. Don't just walk in; call up the branch manager and make an appointment to discuss the various services offered by the bank. If you are just starting out on your own, you might use the same bank branch as your parents or another family member; have them call to make an appointment for you. While your account may initially be small, the manager should be made aware that you are a member of a family with a number of revenue-producing accounts at that

Real life, real answers.

Ted Kranz moved out of his parents' house in southern New Jersey when he graduated from college and began working as a mechanical engineer for Brentline Industries in St. Louis.

Because Ted had never had a checking or savings account in his own name, or established his own credit record, his new landlord required his parents' signatures and an extra two months' rent as a guarantee for the lease. Just starting his working career in a new location, Ted realized he needed a checking account and credit cards in his name. He just didn't know where to go or how to begin.

After Ted discussed his problem with Brentline's personnel director, an appointment was set up for him with a branch manager of the bank at which the company maintained its payroll and general disbursement bank accounts. Ted was given a letter of introduction that included a comment expressing confidence in his career potential with the company.

Ted established a savings account and a checking account with credit-line/overdraft protection of $1,000. The branch manager also approved a Visa bank card for Ted.

As a newcomer to the area, with a new job and no credit history, it is doubtful Ted would have received the credit line and Visa card without the intervention of the personnel director. In their desire to maintain good relations with corporate customers, banks will, upon request, often extend special courtesies and considerations to that customer's employees. It is not necessary for the company to make any guarantees or assume any liabilities on behalf of their employee; a call or letter from a company official is often sufficient to get individual attention.

branch.

An introduction to the bank by a V.I.P. is helpful. If you don't know anyone like that, have an executive or someone in the personnel office of your employer call your employer's local bank to provide an introduction. What you are looking for is some individual recognition that will set you apart from the many others who pass through the bank each day. Having the bank get to know you today sets the stage for it being more willing to help you later, when that might be very important to you.

Open a checking account at the bank. Each week, stop in, deposit a portion of your paycheck into the checking account, and say hello to the bank's staff. When you write checks, make sure there are sufficient funds in the account: do not write any checks that will bounce. The bank may offer "overdraft protection" on checking accounts, so that any checks you write that exceed the balance in your account will be honored up to a certain credit limit. The overdraft amount is set up as an automatic loan the bank will make to you. By all means sign up for this service if they will give it to you. Once you have opened a checking account, you have begun to create your own credit profile in the bank's permanent files.

If possible, you should also start a savings or insured money market account. Setting aside about 10 percent of your income into a savings account is a fundamental step toward financial security.

One way to begin creating a credit history is to take out a small bank loan and repay it on schedule. Even if you have no need for the loan proceeds and it will cost you some money in interest, it will be worth it. Using the balance in your savings account as collateral if necessary, take out a $1,000 loan for a year. To cut your interest costs, put the loan proceeds into an interest-paying account at another bank. When the loan is paid off, you will have made an important positive entry into your credit history at a relatively minor interest cost.

CHARGE ACCOUNTS

Once you have opened up your checking and savings accounts, the next thing to do to establish credit is to open department store charge accounts. Quite often, the criteria for obtaining a department store charge account are more liberal than for other credit-granting organizations. That's because the department stores know that their sales revenue is dependent upon customers having credit cards, and they want your business. If you are granted a credit card, use it wisely. Don't spend money for unnecessary items; avoid impulse buying; exercise control. Do not let your rate of spending increase merely because you are now able to charge your purchases. Make sure you pay your charge accounts in full, when they are due. Don't be late; remember, your charge account records are an important part of your individual credit record.

Department stores, banks, and credit card companies will often send preapproved credit cards or charge account cards to recent college graduates, newlyweds, and home buyers whose home addresses are located in what their marketing people have classified as "the right (higher income) neighborhoods." Credit promotion departments get this information from college yearbooks, wedding announcements, real estate transaction reports, etc. Signing up for one of these cards may be an excellent way to speed up the process of establishing credit, but make certain you read and understand the terms and conditions under which the card will operate.

CREDIT UNIONS

Many companies, large and small, have their own in-house credit unions. While credit unions are subject to special laws and regulations, they may be somewhat easier places to obtain a first loan. The loan committee is usually made up of individuals working by your side who know you and probably live in economic circumstances similar to yours.

CO-SIGNERS

If you are unable to obtain credit on your own, it may be

necessary to find a co-signer—someone with an acceptable credit rating who will take legal responsibility that the loan will be paid off. Parents often co-sign for their children. The important thing is to pay off the loan on time so the lending organization doesn't call upon the co-signer to make good. If the bank calls upon the co-signer because you fall behind or fail to pay off the loan, your credit record will look bad even if the co-signer satisfies the bank.

CREDIT BUREAUS

The national and regional credit bureaus in the United States collect, collate, and distribute credit and financial information on millions and millions of people. Banks, stores, credit card companies, mortgage companies, finance companies—almost every organization you can think of—has a relationship with one or more credit bureaus with whom they exchange information. The credit bureaus also monitor courts (for bankruptcies and judgments), county records offices (for liens against properties), and other sources.

Your credit record is probably on the master computer files of all the credit bureaus, and will remain there, building up a history for all qualified parties to see. According to federal law (the Fair Credit Reporting Act), credit bureaus are permitted to sell the information they have accumulated on you to anyone deciding to extend credit to you, to anyone thinking of hiring you, to anyone trying to sell insurance to you, or anyone else with a legitimate business need for the information. For all practical purposes, you might as well consider your record to be an open book.

Fall behind in payments for your auto loan and it will show up on your credit record. Ignore the dunning letters and it will show up on your credit record.

Not only is your credit record vulnerable to your own acts, you may also become an innocent victim of an error. If some data entry clerk makes a mistake, someone else's credit problem may end up on your record. Your credit record may get an unwarranted black mark because you refused to pay for shoddy or inoperative merchandise. While you may be having your eighth argument in the last four weeks with the store's service manager to get someone over to finally fix or replace a defective appliance, a clerk in their credit department may be putting a stamp on a past due notice to you. Does it happen often? Yes, but you can and should do something about it if you are a victim of a misunderstanding or someone else's error.

It is easy to slip up in making all your payments on time, or to make a mistake and send out a check that bounces. Unfortunately, these occurrences become part of your credit record. They are like tattoos that won't come off. Collect enough of them and you will have seriously impaired your ability to get credit for years to come.

It is wise to review your credit record regularly, and especially before you approach a lending institution for a significant loan. Your records may be maintained by any number of national or regional credit bureaus. Ask your bank for the name and address of the organization it normally uses. Chances are your record will be available at any such organization used by one of your local banks.

You can also call or write to an office of a credit bureau listed in your local Yellow Pages to obtain a copy of your credit record. You may have to pay a small fee for this service, but it will be worthwhile.

TURNED DOWN? SPEAK UP!

Being turned down by one lender does not necessarily mean that you will be turned down somewhere else. Credit approval standards can and do vary from organization to organization, and, surprisingly, even within the same organization. To complicate matters further, the general economic climate may also influence the willingness (and sometimes the ability) of the lending organization to grant loans. You can be certain that lending organizations located in the severely depressed "oil patch" areas of Oklahoma and Texas are operating on a revised and tougher set of lending standards than they did just a few years ago.

If you are turned down for credit, always ask why you were rejected. You might have an opportunity to correct the situation. Perhaps the reasons for your rejection can be straightened out with an explanation; maybe additional information is needed, or a simple clerical error was made. Whatever you do, don't turn tail and run. Insist on knowing the reason for the rejection.

THE FAIR CREDIT REPORTING ACT

If the reason for the rejection lies within the data in your credit report, you have certain legal rights according to the Fair Credit Reporting Act.

Your credit record is compiled by organizations that get their information from others. There is no certainty that the information is accurate or complete. One of the rights you have is to get from the lender who has rejected your application the name, address, and phone number of the credit bureau it used as the source of information. Contact the credit bureau and obtain the information on the report free of charge, including the sources from which their information was obtained. (You will probably have to send the credit bureau a copy of the credit rejection letter you get from the lending institution to obtain the free copy of your credit report.)

If you believe any of the information on the credit report is incorrect, you have the right to tell your side of the story. Within a reasonable period of time, the credit bureau must investigate any information that you dispute. If they find that what you have said is correct, they must correct their report. If their investigation proves that their original information was accurate, the

Real life, real answers.

"Installation and delivery included—only $333.33," the department store ad proclaimed. John and Myra Stone bought the washing machine using the charge account they had with the store. After it was installed, the machine began operating erratically. Despite several visits by service personnel over a period of three months, the washing machine continued to malfunction.

Finally, the Stones advised a member of the store's service department that no further payments would be made until the unit was replaced. However, the store's credit and billing department began sending past due notices. The Stones' calls and complaints seemed to fall on deaf ears. At long last, after repeated calls and letters, the store finally provided a no-charge replacement.

The Stones began making the regular payments on the new washer, but their monthly bills continued to reflect the account as "past due" and added late payment penalties based on the shipping date of the original washer. Resigned to the nonresponsiveness of the store's credit department, the Stones ignored the penalty surcharges and did not attempt to "catch up" on the payments skipped.

Then, much to their surprise, a routine application for another credit card was turned down. The Stones suddenly realized that a situation that had until then seemed only frustrating was now actually affecting their ability to obtain credit from other organizations. They made a personal visit to the store's credit manager with copies of all the pertinent documents and a record of all calls to the store. The credit manager immediately corrected the Stones' account record and canceled all late charges.

At the Stones' insistence, the credit manager also obtained a current copy of the Stones' credit record from the regional credit-reporting service. As they suspected, their alleged "slow pay" was on the record. They insisted (their legal right) that the store immediately take all necessary steps to clear their record and to advise any other organization that had received a copy of the misleading and incorrect credit report.

credit bureau must still allow you to add a written amendment with your side of the story and include it in all their future reports on you.

THE EQUAL CREDIT OPPORTUNITY ACT

This federal law is designed to prohibit discrimination in granting credit on the basis of race, religion, age, sex, or marital status. The reasons for this law are obvious; there is a long, bitter history of exactly this type of discrimination. Unfortunately, some of it still exists, perhaps more subtly than in the past. Because granting credit can be described as a "judgment call," it is difficult for any one individual to prevail in a complaint of this nature unless the personnel of the credit-granting organization have been overtly bigoted in how they have gone about their rejection.

The special problems women once had in obtaining credit from financial institutions had its roots in both male chauvinism and prevailing social and banking customs. It wasn't that women were inherently worse credit risks than men; rather, few women were considered to have independent means of support and income aside from that provided by a husband. If a single woman worked, her status was viewed as a temporary aberration; she would soon marry and retire to the kitchen. If she were a working married woman, she was expected to leave to have children. If she did not, it was supposedly an indication that she was married to a poor earner and her earnings were needed to put food on the table and pay the rent.

Fortunately, the federal Equal Credit Opportunity Act made such discriminatory preconceptions illegal. Although vestiges of the old prejudices may still be found among some lenders, creditworthy women can now obtain credit on their own merits.

If you are convinced that your creditworthiness and credit history justify the amount of credit you are seeking and that your rejection is discrimination-based, contact someone at a high executive level at the credit-granting organization. Indicate that your credit request might have been unfairly treated and that you would like to review the matter in detail with him or her as soon as possible.

If you are correct about your creditworthiness, you will get your meeting and a second chance. If you still end up with a refusal, it might be better to go someplace else for the credit. Filing a complaint with the federal government under this act may make you a real martyr, but heaven knows when you will get the loan you want. Decide upon your priorities and then proceed.

CHAPTER IV

Interest

S imply stated, interest is the rent paid for using other people's money. What isn't so simple are the many different methods by which interest can be calculated, even if the rate of interest seems to be the same. Understanding these methods is an important step in learning how to use credit.

PAYING RENT FOR MONEY

There are three basic components to the calculation of interest cost. Changing one or more of them has a significant impact on the true interest cost:

1. *The amount of principal*; that is, how much is owed at the point in time the interest cost is being calculated.
2. *The period of time* during which interest will be calculated on the principal amount.
3. *The rate of interest* that will be charged on the principal amount owed during the time period.

Most people are aware of the effects and interrelationships of the three components: the more you owe, the greater the interest cost will be; the longer you owe it, the greater the interest cost will be; the higher the interest rate, the greater the interest cost will be. What is least understood is that different methods of interest calculation and different loan repayment plans have an enormous effect upon the final, true interest cost paid. This is true even if it first appears that the principal, time, and interest rate factors are all the same.

THE TRUTH IN LENDING ACT

Under this federal law, lenders are required to clearly disclose (among other things) accurate information regarding the actual cost of the financing. This must be expressed both as a dollar amount and as an annual percentage rate, often referred to as the "APR."

One purpose of this law is to provide consumers with a consistent basis of comparison, making it easier for them to determine from among various credit-granting organizations the one that is offering the best (cheapest) interest rate. Many advertisements now appear in which the APR being offered is as prominently displayed as the price of the item being sold. Unfortunately, the APR does not tell the whole story.

NOT SO SIMPLE INTEREST

Assume you are going to borrow $1,000 at 10 percent to be paid back in one year. Here are some different ways that the interest charge may be calculated.

Simple interest/single payment

This is the least expensive way to borrow money. At the end of the year, you would make one payment to the lender of $1,100, made up of the $1,000 original principal borrowed plus $100 in annual interest ($1,000.00 x 10% x 1 year). You have had the use of the full $1,000 for the entire 12 months.

If, however, you pay off the loan in 12 equal monthly installments over the year, your payment, at the same 10 percent interest rate, would be approximately $87.92 per month or $1,055.04 ($87.92 x 12) over the year. The aggregate amount paid ($1,055.04) under the 12-month installment basis is less than the aggregate $1,100 paid in the single payment example because of the effect of amortization (the reduction of the principal by periodic partial payments).

Under an amortizing loan, once you make the first monthly

payment of $87.92 (which includes the payment of $8.33 in interest on the $1,000 for one month and a partial payment of $79.59 toward the principal), you will then owe a principal balance of only $920.41 ($1,000–$79.59). In the second month, you make your payment of $87.92, but $7.67 is for one month's interest charged on the revised $920.41 principal amount, with $80.25 going toward the principal.

This amortization pattern continues for the full year, with more of each payment going toward reduction of the principal as the amount required for interest declines. Although it may appear that the interest rate is declining, notice that you have the use of a smaller amount of the lender's money each month because you have been paying back part of the principal.

In the first example, you had the entire $1,000 for the full 12 months before you repaid any of it. In the second example, you had less and less of the original $1,000 each month (see page 37), so the aggregate amount of interest paid was less. Even though both loans may be correctly quoted at a 10 percent APR, the interest expense results are quite different.

Discounted interest

With this type of loan, the lender deducts the 10 percent interest ($100) up front and lends you only $900. At the end of the year, you are to repay the lender $1,000 in a single payment. Sounds simple, except that you will have paid $100 in interest to get only $900 of principal. When calculated ($100/$900), this makes the true interest rate you have paid 11.11 percent

Even worse, suppose you take the $900 and agree to make 12 equal monthly payments of $83.33 ($1,000/12) so that at the end of the year your $1,000 loan will be completely paid off. Under these circumstances, the effective interest rate you will have paid would be almost 20 percent. Why? Because as you make the monthly payments, you are reducing (amortizing) the amount of principal you owe each month, but the $100 interest charged was calculated as if you had the entire $1,000 principal for a full year.

Comparison of Outstanding Principal Amount of a $1,000 Loan at 10% for 1 Year Single Payment Loan and 12-Month Amortizing Basis

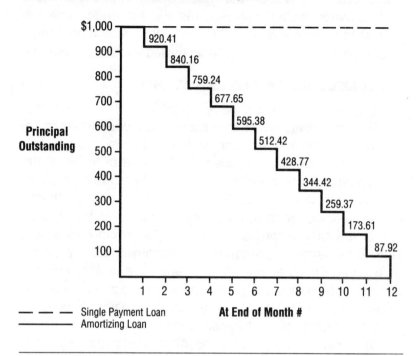

Principal Outstanding

- 920.41
- 840.16
- 759.24
- 677.65
- 595.38
- 512.42
- 428.77
- 344.42
- 259.37
- 173.61
- 87.92

— — — Single Payment Loan
———— Amortizing Loan

At End of Month #

Add-on interest

Another sneaky way of setting the interest rate so that it appears you are getting a bargain is calling it "add-on" interest. Suppose you are offered a 12-month installment loan of $1,000 at a 10 percent add-on rate. Sounds like a fair deal, doesn't it? Let's see how this works out. The lender will add on the $100 interest ($1,000 x 10 percent for one year) to the $1,000 principal he has lent you to arrive at $1,100. The lender divides the $1,100 by 12 to arrive at your monthly payment of $91.67. In reality, the true annual interest rate you are paying on this installment loan is almost 18 percent.

The graph on page 39 indicates that if you are quoted an

"add-on" or "discounted" interest rate, the true annual percentage rate you will pay is almost twice the seemingly cheaper rate quoted. While federal law requires the lender to state the interest to be charged in both a dollar amount and an annual percentage rate, it is still easy to be misled if you aren't careful.

A BALANCE BY ANY OTHER NAME

There is an example on page 40 of a monthly statement covering the activity in a charge account at a department store. The actual amount of financing cost you are charged will depend upon the method used by the store to arrive at the balance upon which the APR is applied to calculate the charge.

The method to be used for calculating the finance charge should be disclosed to you. Usually, it appears on the application for the charge card as well as on the monthly statement itself. For example, a paragraph accompanying an application for a charge card at one department store states that "we calculate the finance charge by applying the periodic rate (the APR divided by 12) to the 'average daily balance' on your account including current transactions."

What this means is that the store takes the beginning balance of your account each day, adds new purchases and subtracts any payments or credits each day, and arrives at a daily closing balance. At the end of the period (usually a month), the store will total up the daily ending balances for the entire period and divide that total by the number of days in that period. The result is your "average daily balance." Using the sample statement on page 40, the total of the 30 daily ending balances during the month of June is $13,100. Dividing that number by 30 gives you an average daily balance of $436.67. At an APR of 18 percent, the finance charge would be $6.55.

Other typical methods of calculating the balance upon which the APR is to be charged follow.

Adjusted balance method

In this method, the balance used for the current interest calcu-

**Comparison of Add-On Rates and Discounted Rates to
True Annual Percentage Rate**

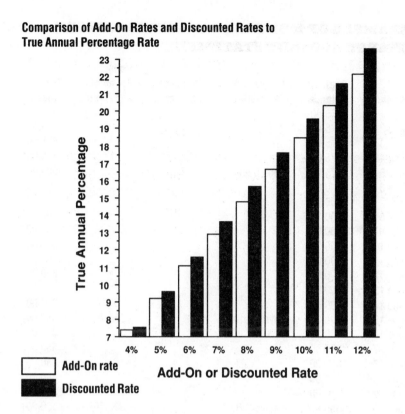

Add-On rate
Discounted Rate

Add-On or Discounted Rate

lation is computed by deducting payments made during the current period from the balance owed at the beginning of the current period. Using the statement on page 40, the adjusted balance is $25 ($475–[$250 + $200]), and the finance charge at an 18 percent APR is 38 cents.

Previous balance method

In this method, the balance used in the current interest calculation is based solely upon the balance at the conclusion of the previous period. Using the sample statement, the previous balance (beginning balance at June 1) is $475, and the finance charge at an 18 percent APR is $7.13.

EXAMPLE OF MONTHLY DEPARTMENT STORE CHARGE ACCOUNT STATEMENT

Month/Day	Beginning Balance	Transaction Description	Add Purchases and Charges	Deduct Payments and Credits	Ending Balance
June 1	475.00				475.00
June 2	475.00				475.00
June 3	475.00				475.00
June 4	475.00				475.00
June 5	475.00	Shoe Dept	125.00		600.00
June 6	600.00				600.00
June 7	600.00				600.00
June 8	600.00				600.00
June 9	600.00				600.00
June 10	600.00				600.00
June 11	600.00				600.00
June 12	600.00				600.00
June 13	600.00				600.00
June 14	600.00				600.00
June 15	600.00	Payment Rec'd		250.00	350.00
June 16	350.00				350.00
June 17	350.00				350.00
June 18	350.00				350.00
June 19	350.00				350.00
June 20	350.00				350.00
June 21	350.00	Payment Rec'd		200.00	150.00
June 22	150.00				150.00
June 23	150.00				150.00
June 24	150.00				150.00
June 25	150.00				150.00
June 26	150.00				150.00
June 27	150.00	Clothing Dept	400.00		550.00
June 28	550.00				550.00
June 29	550.00				550.00
June 30	550.00				550.00

WHEN DOES THE INTEREST METER START RUNNING?

Another factor that will influence the amount of interest you will be charged is when the interest period starts. Some credit card companies start computing interest beginning on the date the credit card transaction is posted on their books. This is not necessarily the date you used the card, but the date when the sales documents sent by the vendor are processed by the credit card company. If the credit card is used for a cash advance, some credit card companies begin computing the interest earlier—as of the date of the cash advance transaction itself. This is the currently advertised practice of the Discover Card.

A Sears store credit card currently allows you 30 days from the billing date to pay the total balance before interest is charged. One internationally recognized bank credit card currently allows you a 25-day grace period from the date of their monthly statement to you before interest is charged. Another well-known credit card company currently begins calculating interest beginning on the date the credit card transaction is posted to their records.

You must read the disclosures regarding interest calculation that appear on both the original application form and the monthly statement of each credit card you have.

WHO SETS THE INTEREST RATE?

Theoretically, interest rates are based upon the supply of and demand for money. This is a gross oversimplification, of course. Interest rates depend upon the combined impact of so many variable factors and forces that the process often makes sense only to college professors and government economists. As far as the average consumer is concerned, interest rates being charged for loans and credit seem very quick to go up and extremely slow to come down, no matter what.

There was a time when the level of risk involved in a loan had a considerable effect on the interest rate charged. The more the risk, the higher the rate. Today, with so many credit record reports, past-history checks, and investigations done beforehand, lending institutions have been minimizing their loan risks by refusing many "marginal" applicants for credit. Thus, once an

Real life, real answers.

I t was an offer that seemed hard to beat. "No money down. No monthly payments for 6 months. Up to 3 years to pay. Only 12 percent APR."

Frank and Fran Lynch spent over two hours selecting $2,000 worth of wall-to-wall carpeting for their apartment, but they didn't spend two minutes reading and understanding the fine print of the installment contract. If they had, they would have realized just how much an ad is allowed to leave out.

While the advertisement said that no payments were due for six months, it did not mean that no interest would be charged for those six months. So, although their carpet was installed on July 1 and the first payment wouldn't be due until the following January 1, they would be charged interest for the $2,000 for those six months at 12 percent. And, since the three-year term of the loan included the initial six-month nonpayment period, the Lynches' payments would be spread out over only the final 30 months of the full 36 months.

Thus, instead of having to pay $66.43 per month for 36 months ($2,391.48 in total), the Lynches paid $82.15 for 30 months ($2,464.50 in total). What looked like a great deal was actually a more expensive way to buy the carpeting than if they had begun payments immediately.

individual has been approved for credit, the risk element has been reduced as a major factor in affecting the interest rate.

The real factors in setting the interest rate are the prime rate (the rate at which the biggest and best corporations can borrow money from banks; published daily in *The Wall Street Journal*); competition among the many credit-granting organizations to make loans; and usury laws (statutes pertaining to the legal maximum interest rates allowed) of the home state of the lending organization.

If you have a good credit history, you should shop for the best interest rate available. Not all banks, credit cards, or loan companies will have the same rate for the same type of loan. You should certainly start your search at the institutions that know you best, but don't ever ask at just one place. Look around. Allow yourself sufficient time for the process. Borrowing in haste is not only an indication of poor money management and lack of planning, it can cost you extra money in interest expenses and other finance charges.

FLOATING RATES

In an attempt to protect themselves from being stuck with low-interest-paying short-term and long-term loans, credit institutions have tied in the interest rate they charge on some loans to various index rates, the most common of which is the prime rate. For example, the interest rate on a loan may be quoted to you at "2 percent over prime," meaning that whatever the prime rate is (say 11 percent), you would be charged 2 percentage points over that rate—or 13 percent. The prime rate may change at any time and without warning owing to money supply factors, general economic conditions, and government policies. If the interest rate on your loan is tied to the prime rate and that rate goes up, the amount of interest you pay will automatically increase as of the day the prime rate increases. If the prime rate goes down, your interest costs will drop accordingly.

In recent years, the prime rate has shown considerable volatility, both up and down. But it always seems that the prime rate increases faster and in bigger chunks than when it is falling. Having an interest rate tied to the prime rate can put enormous strain on your cash flow when you have to allocate more of your income to cover unexpectedly high interest costs. Accepting a loan with a rate tied to the prime may be a necessary but unknown risk. It may also be the only basis on which the lending institution is willing to grant the loan.

You must consider what will happen to your ability to stay current with your loan payments if a floating interest rate increases. If you have serious doubts regarding your ability to meet possible higher interest costs, be very careful before agreeing to such terms.

It is foolish for the average individual to try to outguess the experts regarding which way interest rates will go in the future. If it is probable that increases in your future income will be marginal at best, then try to get a fixed rate and avoid the interest rate gamble. With a fixed interest rate, even one slightly higher than would be available as a floating rate, you know what you will have to pay for the term of your loan. If you are confident that prospects for increasing your earnings are favorable, it may pay you to take the gamble on which way the rates will go in the future and accept a floating rate. Either way, there is no sure thing.

CHAPTER V

Types of loans

Many banks and other financial institutions give fancy names to their various loan packages, but there are only four fundamental types of loans:

1. Secured loans. A secured loan carries with it the pledge of specifically designated collateral (house, car, jewelry, stock certificate, or other valuable asset) to which the borrower (and/or any co-signers or guarantors) has legal title. This collateral is pledged as security that the loan and interest will be repaid.

2. Unsecured loans. An unsecured loan does not have any specific collateral designated as security for the payment of the loan. However, in the event of a loan default, the lender may take legal action that can place any and all of the borrower's assets (and/or that of any co-signers or guarantors) in jeopardy.

3. Demand loans. When you negotiate a demand loan, you are giving the financial institution the right to demand repayment or "call the loan" at any time. However, once the institution has agreed to grant a demand loan (usually only to important and financially secure customers), it will rarely call the loan except under extraordinary circumstances. Although interest is usually paid on a regular schedule, the principal balance of a demand loan can remain outstanding for quite some time with no repayment so long as the creditworthiness of the borrower satisfies the lender.

4. Time loans. In a time loan, the date when the complete repayment of the loan is due is specified when the loan is first negotiated. Interest is usually paid on a regular schedule. A time loan may also require regular payments of a portion of the principal balance during the life of the loan.

Demand loans and time loans can be either secured or unsecured, depending upon the terms and conditions of the loan.

INSTALLMENT LOANS

Installment loans represent by far the largest category of time loans taken out by consumers. Automobiles, major appliances, and practically anything else can be financed using an installment loan. Consumers sign up for them because they are relatively easy to get and the fixed monthly payment is a convenient method of repayment. Financial institutions like them because they are usually very profitable.

With some effort, you might be able to save money the next time you are faced with taking out an installment loan. You now know that the simple interest/single payment loan is the least expensive loan. With some smart negotiating, you may be able to arrange for a bank loan usually set up as an installment loan to be processed instead as a simple interest/single payment loan. It won't be easy to do; you will get lots of resistance, but it is well worth trying.

Assume you are buying a car and intend to finance $10,000 over 36 months. You have a good credit record, so you stop into your regular bank to discuss the loan with the branch manager. The bank is willing to give you 36 months to pay and charge you 15 percent APR interest on an installment loan basis, requiring a $346.65 monthly payment. So far you haven't and shouldn't have mentioned the single payment plan; you don't want the banker to bump up his interest rate. Once the bank has committed to the dollar amount, interest rate, and term of the loan, you can then try for the single payment method, but with a twist.

Tell the banker you are willing to pay the loan off over 36 months at the 15 percent APR interest the bank has quoted, but you want it structured as a *single payment loan that allows monthly payments*. You will pay $277.78 per month toward the principal ($10,000/36) plus interest at 15 percent APR on the principal balance each month. After the banker shakes his head in amazement, you argue that since the bank has approved your creditworthiness for $10,000 over 36 months at 15 percent APR, there is no additional risk to the bank. Why not structure the loan as you have requested? What's the big deal?

The chart on page 48 compares the results of the two different loan types. If you get to do it your way, you will save $167.30 in interest over the three years (that's extra profit the bank won't make). For the first 17 months, your weekly payment of principal plus interest will be higher than it would have been under the installment plan, although that difference will get smaller each month. For the last 19 months, your monthly payments will be less than that required by the installment method. If you can handle the slightly larger payments in the earlier months, the single payment loan is your best bet.

Banks don't offer single payment loans and don't want to talk about them. One banker acknowledged that it is was a better deal for consumers but said that "our computers aren't programmed to handle that type of repayment plan, and wouldn't be until competition from other banks forced them to." Since most consumers don't take the time to learn how they are being taken for extra money, the banks certainly won't make it any easier.

PERSONAL LOANS

Some institutions, after review and approval of your application and credit history, will grant you a "revolving line of credit" up to a certain amount. For example, if you get an approved line of up to $3,000, you don't have to take all of it at once, just when and as you need funds. These loans are often accompanied by a supply of special checks. When you write a special check

INSTALLMENT LOAN VS. SINGLE PAYMENT LOAN

| | | Installment loan basis | | | | Single payment loan | | |
| | Principal | Monthly payment to | | | Principal | Monthly payment to | | |
Month	Balance	Principal	Interest	Total	Balance	Principal	Interest	Total
1	10,000.00	221.65	125.00	346.65	10,000.00	277.78	125.00	402.78
2	9,775.35	224.42	122.23	346.65	9,722.22	277.78	121.53	399.31
3	9,553.93	227.23	119.42	346.65	9,443.44	277.78	118.04	395.82
4	9,326.70	230.07	116.58	346.65	9,165.06	277.78	114.57	392.35
5	9,046.63	232.94	113.71	346.65	8,887.88	277.78	111.10	388.88
6	8,863.69	235.85	110.80	346.65	8,610.10	277.78	107.66	385.44
7	8,627.84	238.80	107.85	346.65	8,332.32	277.78	104.15	381.93
8	8,389.04	241.79	104.86	346.65	8,054.54	277.78	100.68	378.46
9	8,147.25	244.81	101.84	346.65	7,776.76	277.78	97.21	374.99
10	7,902.44	247.87	98.78	346.65	7,498.98	277.78	93.74	371.52
11	7,654.57	250.97	95.68	346.65	7,221.20	277.78	90.27	368.05
12	7,403.60	254.10	92.55	346.65	6,843.42	277.78	86.79	364.57
13	7,149.50	257.28	89.37	346.65	6,665.64	277.78	83.32	361.10
14	6,892.22	260.50	86.15	346.65	6,387.86	277.78	79.85	357.63
15	6,631.72	263.75	82.90	346.65	6,110.08	277.78	76.38	354.16
16	6,367.97	267.05	79.60	346.65	5,832.30	277.78	72.90	350.68
17	6,100.92	270.39	76.26	346.65	5,554.52	277.78	69.43	347.21
18	5,830.53	273.77	72.88	346.65	5,276.74	277.78	65.96	343.74
19	5,556.76	277.19	69.46	346.65	4,998.96	277.78	62.49	340.27
20	5,279.57	280.66	65.99	346.65	4,721.18	277.78	59.01	336.79
21	4,998.91	284.16	62.49	346.65	4,443.40	277.78	55.54	333.32
22	4,714.75	287.72	58.93	346.65	4,165.62	277.78	52.07	329.85
23	4,427.03	291.31	55.34	346.65	3,887.84	277.78	48.60	326.38
24	4,135.72	294.95	51.70	346.65	3,610.06	277.78	45.13	322.91
25	3,840.77	298.64	48.01	346.65	3,332.28	277.78	41.65	319.43
26	3,542.13	302.37	44.28	346.65	3,054.50	277.78	38.18	315.96
27	3,239.76	306.15	40.50	346.65	2,776.72	277.78	34.71	312.49
28	2,933.61	309.98	36.67	346.65	2,498.94	277.78	31.24	309.02
29	2,623.63	313.85	32.80	346.65	2,221.16	277.78	27.76	305.54
30	2,309.78	317.78	28.87	346.65	1,943.38	277.78	24.29	302.07
31	1,992.00	321.75	24.90	346.65	1,665.60	277.78	20.82	298.60
32	1,670.25	325.77	20.88	346.65	1,387.82	277.78	17.35	295.13
33	1,344.48	329.84	16.81	346.65	1,110.04	277.78	13.88	291.66
34	1,014.64	333.97	12.68	346.65	832.26	277.78	10.40	288.18
35	680.67	338.14	8.51	346.65	554.48	277.78	6.93	284.71
36	342.53	_342.53_	_4.12_	_346.65_	277.70	_277.70_	_3.47_	_281.17_
Totals		10,000.00	2,479.40	12,479.40		10,000.00	2,312.10	12,312.10

against your credit line, the bank automatically charges your preapproved loan account for the check amount. You pay interest only on the total amount you owe, not on the amount of the authorized credit line.

Personal loans, including lines of credit, are usually given for a specific length of time—one to three years—although they may be renewed during or at the expiration of the initial loan term.

An unsecured personal loan requires an above average credit rating on the part of the borrower, as it is probably the riskiest of all loans made by a financial institution. It is also quite expensive, with an interest rate that is usually 3 to 5 percent above the prime rate, and subject to immediate change as the prime rate moves up and down. Banks will sometimes grant exceptionally good and/or important customers special, below-market rates that are not available to ordinary customers.

Secured personal loans require you to give the bank some form of collateral as security. The collateral may be your house, stocks and bonds, certificates of deposit, an art collection, a car, or anything else the financial institution believes would have sufficient market value in the event it has to seize and sell the property to pay off the loan. Some items of property such as art collections or stamp collections might be placed in the financial institution's possession for safekeeping while the loan is outstanding. Secured loans usually are made at somewhat lower interest rates than unsecured loans.

Secured and unsecured personal loans may be paid off on a term basis, with a specified minimum of principal payments at the end of each month. The minimum payment is based on a percentage of the loan balance at the end of each month and/ or the term of the loan. The borrower has the option of paying more than the minimum required payment. Interest is charged at the agreed upon rate based on the daily loan balance, and is usually paid monthly.

HOME EQUITY LOANS

This loan is a variation of the secured personal loan described above. Using the equity (the difference between the current market value of the real estate minus any debt owed on that real estate) in your house as collateral, a home equity loan (usually available for up to 80 percent of the equity value) may be set up as a revolving line of credit or as a fixed-term second mortgage (usually for no more than 10 years). Unfortunately, too many lenders are heavily promoting home equity loans to consumers as the greatest thing since sliced bread.

Under the 1986 federal tax code revisions, restrictions regarding the deductibility of interest paid on consumer loans went into effect. For tax years beginning in 1991, entirely new rules will become effective. The deductibility of interest paid on qualifying residential loans may still be deductible depending on your individual circumstances. A qualified tax expert should be consulted. As of this writing, borrowers are using home equity loans to pay credit card bills, for medical expenses, vacations, cars—all sorts of things. So far, the Internal Revenue Service rarely has contested the deductibility of interest paid on home equity loans used for non-house-related expenditures.

But the tax deductibility of the home equity loan may turn out to be a phantom benefit. There are substantial up-front costs connected with this type of loan, including application, appraisal, title search, recording, closing, and other fees. You may pay more in fees than the tax break you get on the interest. Interest rates charged on home equity loans vary between $1\frac{1}{2}$ and 3 percent over the floating prime rate, although some fixed-rate arrangements are available.

The equity in their homes is usually the largest single financial asset of most American families. It should not be put at risk unnecessarily. Besides being a valuable financial asset, the house probably contributes to your family's stability, way of life, and security. Using it as collateral for a home equity loan makes it vulnerable to foreclosure and loss. Don't risk your house on a home equity loan unless the loan is absolutely necessary.

STUDENT/EDUCATION LOANS

With the cost of college averaging about $10,000 and running as high as $25,000 a year, meeting education expenses is a major undertaking for most American families. Increases in tuition costs have outstripped the means of all but the wealthiest families.

There are public and privately funded scholarships for a variety of schools and students. Federal and state grant and loan programs are available to qualified applicants, usually at low and/or subsidized interest rates. If you want to explore the various forms of financial aid available, another *Real life, real answers* guide, *How to pay for your child's college education*, is a good place to start.

Some families still need to borrow money to make up the shortfall between the actual educational expenses and the support from the aid and subsidized loan programs. For those families, the home equity loan is usually the only loan that can provide the large amounts of cash required over the full period of college education.

INSURANCE POLICY LOANS

Certain life insurance policies accumulate a cash value that is available for borrowing from the insurance company. The longer the policy has been in existence, the greater the accumulated cash value. The policy document specifies the amount of cash value per thousand dollars of policy face value on different policy anniversary dates. The interest rate to be charged on loans is also specified in the policy.

Usually the interest rate is substantially below rates charged by banks. No credit check is necessary if you borrow against the policy. If the policy has been in force for a number of years, it may represent a substantial pool of money. However, when you borrow against the cash value of an insurance policy, you are reducing the proceeds to be paid by the policy in the event of your death prior to loan repayment. Because you purchased life insurance for the specific purpose of protecting your family's financial security in the event of your death, borrowing against the policy should be done only as a last resort.

MARGIN BORROWING

Stockbrokers will lend money to their customers through a "margin account," wherein the market value of qualified securities owned by those customers (and kept in the custody of the brokerage firm) serve as collateral for the loan. The maximum amount to be borrowed is subject to a formula based on not more than 50 percent of the value of listed stocks, 90 percent of the value of federal government securities, and 70 percent of the value of corporate bonds that will be pledged as the collateral.

Individual brokerage firms may have their own in-house rules governing such margin accounts. In the event the market value of the securities pledged falls below a certain point, you may be required to immediately pay off some or all of the loan and/or increase the amount of collateral. Failure to do so subjects the securities to immediate sale by the brokerage firm to bring the margin account into compliance.

The interest rate charged is based on a special type of securities industry interest rate called a "brokers call rate," (published daily in *The Wall Street Journal*). The brokers call rate is usually below the prime rate, and margin loans are priced some 1 to 3 percent over the brokers call rate.

MORTGAGES

A would-be home owner is usually faced with one of the most difficult financial challenges in his or her life. Substantial amounts of money must be saved up for the down payment, closing costs, and move-in expenses. The problems of finding a desirable home, then selecting and qualifying for an affordable mortgage, seem almost insurmountable. *How to buy your first home*, also in the *Real life, real answers* series, is a good source of basic information for first-time buyers.

It is normal for people buying a home to stretch themselves financially for a few years, postponing vacations, nursing the old car through another winter or two, in order to meet the financial demands of home ownership. The more you save up in cash for a down payment (and to cover closing costs), the better house you can buy.

While 20 to 25 percent of a borrower's income for monthly debt payments is the usual maximum that most lenders will allow, they will raise that limit to 36 percent if it includes mortgage payments. That *doesn't* mean that mortgage payments should be 16 percent, 11 percent, or 36 percent of your income. What it does mean is that the lower your other debt obligations are, the better your chances will be of getting approved for a larger mortgage.

Mortgages come with fixed interest rates and variable interest rates, and for varying terms (usually 15, 20, or 30 years). The shorter the length of the mortgage, the higher the monthly payment, although substantially less total interest will be paid out over the life of the mortgage.

In a fixed-rate mortgage, the interest rate and the monthly mortgage payment remain constant for the life of the mortgage. In variable-rate mortgages, frequently called adjustable-rate mortgages (ARMs), the interest rate is usually tied to changes in some other benchmark short-term interest rate, such as the rate on one-year U.S. Treasury bills. Normally, ARMs initially have lower interest rates than fixed-rate mortgages, thus offering home buyers the opportunity to get a bigger mortgage or a larger home for a given amount of monthly payment. The risk is that as time goes by, the amount of the monthly mortgage payment on an ARM will go up if the benchmark interest rate goes up. Of course, the benchmark rate can come down, thereby reducing the monthly mortgage payment.

Real life, real answers.

S tan Carey believed the easiest way a person of modest means could make a fortune in the stock market was by using "leverage"—getting the most action possible out of a limited amount of capital resources.

Using all $30,000 of his savings plus $20,000 from a home equity loan, Stan bought $50,000 of several stocks on the New York Stock Exchange for cash. By putting those stocks up as collateral with his broker, he was able to buy, on margin, an additional $25,000 of stock, bringing his total market investment to $75,000. As the market continued to rise over the next few months, his stocks increased in market value to $95,000.

Instead of taking some of his profits and/or reducing his margin loan, Stan, on the strength of the increased value of the stocks, bought an additional $15,000 of stock on margin. He was now in debt to the broker for $40,000, which was secured by $95,000 worth of stock. He also still owed $20,000 to the bank on the home equity loan.

When the market suddenly declined sharply, Stan's stocks dropped in value. Within two days, their market value fell to $70,000, considerably less than was needed as collateral for his $40,000 margin account. When the broker called, requesting additional collateral, Stan managed to scrape together sufficient cash to meet that margin call and avoid the broker having to sell some of the pledged stock to reduce the margin debt.

During the next week, the market continued its precipitous decline. When the broker called for more collateral, Stan was unable to come up with any. The broker was forced to sell Stan's stocks into a rapidly dropping market. But, because the market dropped so far so fast, the money the stock brought in was insufficient to completely pay off Stan's margin borrowing.

In the end, Stan still owed $5,000 on his margin debt and $20,000 on the home equity loan. All his savings had been lost. Stan Carey had learned the hard way that leverage works in both directions.

There are a number of different interest rate change formulas under which an ARM may be written. Under some, the interest rate remains fixed for a short period (say one to three years) before being subject to change; in others, the rate is adjusted annually. Usually, the maximum increase or decrease an ARM interest rate can have in one year or over the life of the mortgage is limited ("capped") by the mortgage contract terms. One desirable feature in an ARM is a "conversion clause" which, for a fee, allows you the option to convert to a fixed rate at specified times during the duration of the mortgage.

Most mortgage lenders require "points" to be paid as a surcharge on the amount of the mortgage. In a way, this is merely additional interest, paid in advance and disguised by another name. A point equals 1 percent of the mortgage; thus paying three points on a $100,000 mortgage means paying 3 percent or $3,000 to the lender up front at closing.

The amount of points charged by a lender may vary depending on whether it is an adjustable-rate or fixed mortgage. You should require the lender to provide you with an APR calculation of all mortgage proposals after giving consideration to both the stated interest rate and the impact of any points on the final interest cost calculation. You can then determine which mortgage has the lowest effective rate. According to one rule of thumb, every $1\frac{1}{2}$ points you pay up front is equal to approximately $\frac{1}{4}$ of 1 percent on the mortgage interest rate. Thus paying 3 points on a 10 percent mortgage is about equal to the same mortgage at $10\frac{1}{2}$ percent with no points. If you have trouble coming up with the up-front money for points, you might want to counter with an offer to pay a slightly higher interest rate.

Because mortgage rates do change over time, you want to be in a position to take advantage of a favorable situation after you have taken out a mortgage. If you have an ARM or a fixed-rate mortgage at a high rate and the current rates are lower, you may wish to refinance. No matter what mortgage type you have, you want a clause that permits you to refinance the mortgage with no penalty, or at least a minimal penalty. Given the various legal and closing costs involved in refinancing a mortgage, a decrease of at least 2 percent in the prevailing mortgage rates from what you are currently paying is usually necessary before it makes financial sense.

CHAPTER VI

Auto loans

A uto loans are probably the most common type of install-ment loans and are among the easiest to get. Today's lifestyle requires almost every family to own at least one car, and, with the average car price in the $10,000 to $12,000 range, a four- or five-year auto loan is needed by most. If you'll spend half as much time getting the best deal on an auto loan as you do kicking the tires, checking out the stereo system, and admiring the upholstery, you will definitely save a great deal of money.

HAVE WE GOT A DEAL FOR YOU

Buying a car on time involves two different, but related, opera-tions. The first involves selecting the car and the dealer and negotiating the lowest purchase price. The second involves se-lecting the method of financing and negotiating the lowest rate and most favorable terms.

An auto loan is an installment-type loan with the car pledged as collateral. That means you make a monthly payment, which includes principal and interest, over the term of the loan, and the lending organization has a security interest in the car until the debt is paid in full. If you fall behind in your payments, the lender has the legal right to repossess the car, sell it, and apply the proceeds toward what you owe.

GIVING THE DEALER SOME EXTRA PROFIT

Many car dealers make an extra profit when they sell you a car on an installment plan they have arranged.

Here's how it can work. Dealers usually have working arrangements with several financial institutions, including banks, to which they will sell your automobile loan. Not only can the interest rates vary among the different institutions, but the rate of interest will also be influenced by any repayment guarantee the dealer gives to the financial institution regarding your auto loan.

Let's assume you select a car and negotiate a cash price of $13,500. The dealer allows you a $3,500 trade-in on your old clunker, leaving you a $10,000 balance to be financed. (For the sake of simplicity, we will not concern ourselves with life and accident insurance, sales tax, and title and registration transfer costs.) The dealer quotes you a $10,000 loan for four years at 12 percent, which equals 48 monthly payments of $263.34. Over the full term of the loan, you will pay a total of $12,640.32, including $2,640.32 in interest. When the dealer delivers your completed retail installment contract to the financial institution, the institution will give the dealer $10,000 in cash, completing the dealer's part of the transaction. You will make your monthly payments to the financial institution.

Suppose, however, that one of the banks with which the dealer works is charging only 11 1/4 percent interest. The dealer then can sell your 12 percent installment contract to that bank at a discount. As a result, the dealer gets a check for $10,141.29, which includes the original $10,000 in principal plus an extra profit of $141.29, which is the value today of the interest difference generated over four years between the 12 percent rate you are paying and the 11 1/4 percent rate the dealer gets. This extra profit made by the dealer could have been saved had you shopped for your own loan.

A dealer may also sell the financing contract on a nonrecourse basis (if you don't pay, the dealer has no financial responsibility to the financial institution), or on a with recourse basis (if you don't pay, the dealer has to pay off the loan balance and repossess the car). If the dealer is willing to accept the risk of a with recourse basis, he can get an even lower interest rate and make more financing profit on the transaction. If the dealer were to get a rate of $10^3/_4$ percent on the above transaction by selling your loan on a with recourse basis, he would make an extra profit of $237.02 over and above the profit made on the sale of the car itself.

A clever auto salesman will, in the course of his sales pitch, ask if you intend to pay cash or finance the car purchase. If you respond that you intend to finance, he will ask you some innocuous questions regarding your background and how much you can afford in monthly payments. Using the monthly payment data and a quick, unofficial estimate of your credit-worthiness, the salesman can figure out how much financing he can get for you at various interest rates. By focusing on the monthly payment, the salesman remains almost totally in control of the selling process instead of the other way around. You have given him the ammunition to peg the highest price you will pay for a car, perhaps allowing him to resell your installment contract and make an extra financing profit as well. The moral: always negotiate with the auto dealer as if you were going to be a cash buyer.

Only after you have negotiated the final cash price should you discuss financing alternatives. If you intended all along to finance, you should already know what you can afford and the terms you can get elsewhere. Only then can you compare and evaluate the rates offered by the dealer.

LOW, LOW DEALS ON AUTOMOBILE CREDIT

Periodically, many automobile manufacturers offer extremely low financing rates for the purchase of certain model cars. Typically, the deal offers you the alternative of a low interest rate for a two-year installment contract, or a cash rebate. Should you take the rebate and use available market rate financing, or should you accept the manufacturer's special low rate? You need to do some figuring before you decide.

A two-year, 2.9 percent APR installment loan on $10,500 requires a monthly payment of $450.84 and a total payout of $10,820.16 (including $320.16 in interest) over the loan term. A two-year, 10½ percent APR bank rate installment loan on $10,000 (the price after deducting a $500 rebate) requires a monthly payment of $463.76 and a total payout of $11,130.25 (including $1,130.25 in interest). Although there is a big difference in the APR and total interest paid ($310.09), the difference in your monthly payment is relatively small.

Because the special interest rate offers are usually for two-year loans only, the monthly payment will be higher than a four-year loan at regular interest rates. A $10,000 loan for four years at 10½ percent requires a monthly payment of $256.03, considerably less than either two-year alternative. Even though the aggregate amount paid of $12,289.44 ($256.03 x 48) is much higher, if the struggle to make the larger monthly payments of the shorter term puts too much strain on your budget, you might not have any choice. Before you decide, you must compute the monthly payment and interest costs of all alternatives, then make the decision about what best suits your individual financial situation.

Sometimes an automobile dealer will advertise 0 percent financing for cars purchased from him (such offers are usually made by a dealer and are not part of the automobile manufacturer's special interest programs). You are old enough to know there is no such thing as "a free lunch"; the same holds true for 0 percent interest. You have seen in the above examples that normal interest costs on a $10,000 auto loan for two or more years can total well over $1,000. No dealer is going to absorb those costs out of his own pocket. The way the dealer compensates for his 0 percent interest offer is to charge more for the car than he would in normal circumstances. You can be sure that the car now selling for $10,000 at 0 percent interest could have been purchased from the dealer for well over $1,000 less *before* the 0 percent interest offer (and probably after the program as well).

Suppose you buy a car for $10,000 at 0 percent, with the loan to be paid out over two years. You agree to pay $416.67 per month for 24 months ($10,000/24). The dealer can take that installment contract and sell it to the bank, as described above. If the current bank rate for auto loans is 10½ percent, then your contract to pay $416.67 for 24 months is worth $8,984.60 in a lump sum today. The dealer will get that amount of cash when he delivers your installment contract.

More than likely, your new car could normally have been purchased for a lot less than $10,000. When you agreed to that price, you were effectively paying interest costs that were loaded into the inflated selling price. The next time a dealer offers you 0 percent financing on a car, go to another dealer and see what kind of price you can get for the same car without the 0 percent financing gimmick. Only when you have cash prices from both dealers and know the bank financing rates available can you make a meaningful comparison as to which is the better deal for you.

HOW LONG TO PAY

It is now possible to finance a new car purchase over a five-year term rather than the 24 to 48 months that were standard until recently. Used cars can also be purchased on the installment basis but most lenders will not extend the same terms as they would on a new car. But extending the term of an auto loan (or any installment loan) in order to reduce the monthly payment is an expensive alternative. Here is a comparison based on financing $10,000 at 11 percent APR over various terms.

Term	Monthly Payment	Total Repaid	Interest Expense
2 years	$466.07	$11,185.68	$1,185.68
3 years	$327.39	$11,786.04	$1,786.04
4 years	$258.45	$12,405.60	$2,405.60
5 years	$217.42	$13,045.20	$3,045.20

As you can see, doubling the term from two years to four years does not cut your monthly payment in half, but it does double your total interest expense. In the above example, each additional year adds approximately $600 in extra interest costs to the total repaid.

BUY OR LEASE?

Leasing was once almost exclusively an option chosen by corporations and individuals in certain occupations (doctors, traveling salesmen, and others in a position to write off most of the lease cost as a business expense). But it is now used as an alternative to financing a car by many ordinary consumers. Automobile leases are generally written for terms of three years or more. Greatly simplified, the automobile lease works as follows.

The dealer and the customer sign a lease covering a specific vehicle and optional equipment chosen by the customer. The current selling price of the car, minus a predetermined and agreed upon estimate of the car's residual wholesale value at the expiration of the lease, establishes a net auto value upon which the lease is priced. An interest cost is added to this net value (similar to the interest charged on regular automobile financing) for the length of the lease. The total of the interest cost and the net auto value are paid over the life of the lease, usually in equal monthly installments. (A down payment and/or security deposit is sometimes required; this might take the form of a certain number of months' rent paid in advance.)

Leases often specify a maximum mileage per year or per lease term. Exceed those limits and you pay a hefty per-mile surcharge. A maintenance option clause may be available where, for a fixed price, the dealer will take care of all routine maintenance, oil changes, tire replacements, tuneups, etc., over the life of the lease. If your mileage is not expected to be out of the ordinary, it is probably cheaper not to accept this option and pay for those expenses when and as incurred. However, it may be more convenient to take it because you will probably get a loaner car to use while the car is being serviced.

Some leases are "closed-ended," meaning the lessee (the customer) has no additional financial obligation to the lessor at the end of the lease if the residual, wholesale used-car market value of the car when the lease is finished is less than what was projected at the time the lease was negotiated. If the lease is "open-ended," the lessee may have a financial obligation for part or all of any such difference. The monthly lease cost for a closed-ended lease may be a bit more expensive than for an open-ended lease since the dealer is taking the gamble on the car's future residual market value.

Usually, the lessee has an option to buy the car at the conclusion of the lease for a price equal to the residual value as originally projected by a closed-ended contract. Some individuals deliberately have the dealer set the residual value low, pay a higher monthly charge (which they write off as a business expense), then buy the car at that extra-low price.

It can be difficult making a direct comparison between the true costs of leasing an auto and purchasing that very same auto on the installment loan basis. Even comparing the monthly payments under each method isn't enough because the residual value, interest rate used, security deposit requirements, etc., all have an effect. Excluding the possible tax advantages to leasing, if any, it is fairly safe to conclude that leasing is at least as expensive as borrowing to buy the car.

While you pay sales tax up front on the entire purchase price of a car you buy, and the sales tax is stretched out over the life of a lease, you will be paying additional sales tax on the interest cost that has been included as part of the monthly lease cost.

Still, if you have just about used up all your available credit, you might find it easier to get an automobile lease approved than an auto loan, especially if lease approval rests with the dealer. It won't be any easier for you to make the monthly payments on time, but you will get the new car you want.

CHAPTER VII

Credit cards

I n today's cashless society, practically anything and everything can be charged on a credit card. You don't even have
to show your credit card; just order over the phone and give your
credit card number. The entire process is so easy that the only
financial shock you feel is when the monthly credit card statements arrive and need to be paid. Every time you use your credit
card you have borrowed money and pledged to pay it back.

CONVENIENT TOOL OR BUDGET BREAKER?

The simple truth is that many people forget they can afford to
use either their limited cash assets or their credit card, but *not
both*. They choose to ignore the fact that every time they use a
credit card, they are committing some of their available cash. It's
different when you open your wallet and hand money to some
cashier; you can see the wallet getting thinner. When you use
your credit card, the wallet doesn't seem to be getting thinner,
but it really is. Once money is spent, either through a credit card
or cash, you have less available to spend without going into
debt.

In a way, plastic credit cards are as psychologically decep-
tive as the chips used in a gambling casino. When you toss
down your chips at the roulette wheel or craps table, it may not
seem as if you are risking real money. If you placed your bets
using real dollar bills, you would be more aware of the money
you were risking (and probably losing).

There is nothing inherently wrong in having a credit card or two. Most, if not all, problems associated with credit card use stem from the lack of self-discipline and control on the part of the credit card holder. Credit cards offer convenience and safety (no need to carry large amounts of cash with you). And for some tasks, such as renting a car or getting immediate cash advances, they are practically indispensable.

Credit cards are usually issued on the basis of an application form you and/or your spouse fill out and sign. The approval criteria for each different credit card vary considerably with the policy and standards of each card issuer and the type of credit card. The credit card is issued in the name of the primary applicant(s) upon whose earnings and credit history the credit approval decision is made. Upon the written request of the primary applicant(s), additional cards may be issued to other family members (sometimes for an extra fee), but the primary applicant(s) will remain liable for payment of all charges made on those extra cards.

Remember that interest rates charged on credit card balances are almost always among the highest. Using a credit card for purchases you know you will have to pay off on an installment basis is wasting money. It is far better to try to negotiate a bank or credit union loan at a more favorable interest rate to pay for such purchases.

SINGLE-PURPOSE CARDS

Department stores, gasoline companies, telephone companies, auto rental agencies, your neighborhood drugstore—in fact, hundreds of thousands of business organizations issue their own single-purpose cards through which you are extended credit and encouraged to purchase goods and services from their businesses. The cards are not intended to be usable or acceptable at other retailers; their purpose is to expand the sales of the card-issuing organization and no others. (However, it is not unusual to find retailers who haven't issued you a credit card but are quite willing to extend you credit if you have a competitor's credit card.)

Some department stores have set up a two-tier credit card system—one type offers the customer the opportunity to pay the charge account balance in full within a specified number of days of the billing date to avoid all finance (interest) charges; the other is for making major purchases (appliances, furniture, etc.) with small monthly payments, including interest, spread over a period of time.

Single purpose cards are almost always free, requiring only an application, if that, to get one.

GENERAL-PURPOSE CARDS

The best known of these cards are the American Express card, the Diners Club card and the Carte Blanche card. Originally thought of primarily as travel and entertainment cards to be used by salespeople and business executives while traveling, these cards are now used to charge practically everything. They also offer certain fringe benefits such as travel and baggage insurance, car rental insurance, a phone number to call for help and information while away from home, etc. Annual membership fees are charged for the use of such cards.

There is usually no interest, finance, or late charge if the monthly balance appearing on the statement is paid in full within a specified number days (typically 25 or 30) of the statement date. If the account balance is not paid within the time allotted, late charges, delinquency fees, and interest are charged, the combined effect of which can bring the interest expense to the equivalent of over 20 percent APR. Delinquency will also cause fairly prompt cancellation of the card and possible embarrassment when a vendor, after checking with a central computer source for approval on the charge you are attempting to make, advises you that he has been instructed to retain your card.

While theoretically the cards have no stated credit limit, the credit card company monitors the level of charges made on the card. If a large dollar amount accumulates during a month and that charge pattern seems out of the ordinary based on the past usage of the card, the credit card company may verify, via phone, your ability to handle this new, higher level of charges and/or refuse to permit further charges.

With use over time, it is possible to establish a much higher line of credit on the card—the more dollars you charge and repay promptly each month, the more you will be able to charge on that card in the future. This can get some people in over their heads because it becomes increasingly easy to build up a bigger and bigger charge balance without the discipline of a third party to say "Stop! You've reached our and your limit!"

Most general-purpose cards have a monthly payment installment plan option. In the case of American Express, this option may be used only for airline, train, or bus tickets, and cruises and travel packages charged through certain vendors. This repayment plan option is activated at your request by the vendor at the time the purchase is put on an American Express card. Your monthly statement will then differentiate between regular charges and those on the installment plan. It will also provide you with various payment alternatives, and information about interest costs, finance charges, etc.

In the case of Diners Club, you sign up for the Club Plus option after six months' membership in the club. Based on your history with Diners Club and the results of a credit report, Diners Club will establish an approved, installment plan credit limit for you. There are no restrictions on what may be paid off via the installment plan. Once approved for Club Plus, you may invoke the installment plan option by returning to Diners Club certain appropriately filled-out forms (coupons) received with your monthly statement. These forms advise the card company of the items or balance you wish to put on the Club Plus installment payment plan.

The credit card companies will set the monthly minimum payment to be made against the installment balance. You must pay that minimum, but you have an option to pay any larger amount you wish. Interest at the then current rate is charged on the unpaid balance. The quoted installment rate at American Express in July 1989 was 20.4 percent APR; the rate at Diners Club was 17.3 percent APR. These rates can change at any time, as can the definition of the date upon which the credit card company will begin calculating interest, finance charges, and late fees.

There are also special general-purpose cards, such as the American Express Gold Card, which have a higher membership fee and additional fringe benefits. When arranged through a bank of your choice, they also have a higher dollar credit limit and permit you to withdraw or borrow cash. A credit report will be drawn on you to establish your creditworthiness. These premium cards were designed to offer some of the features of the competitive bank credit cards described below.

BANK CREDIT CARDS

While most people and vendors universally recognize the singular trade names of Visa and MasterCard, in reality these cards are issued by thousands of individual banks in cooperative credit card marketing and financial systems. These cards permit your local bank to participate in the credit card business on an international basis. Suppose Small Bank USA attempted to issue credit cards in its own name, which it hoped would be honored by retailers in Tokyo, Calcutta, Hollywood, or East Podunk. It is doubtful their cards would be accepted in those places. Instead, because each local bank issues a credit card under an internationally known and accepted trade name, it is able to participate and make money in the profitable credit card business.

Bank credit cards can sometimes put a welcome local context into dealing with a credit card company. Rather than deal with a disembodied voice at the other end of an "800" phone number, you can usually take a Visa or MasterCard problem to someone sitting at a desk in the issuing bank's local branch. That person may in turn have to call an "800" number customer service center, but at least you will have been able to show a bank representative the appropriate receipts, canceled checks, or documents; the representative may then help you get your message across. The availability of such local services varies among banks.

Each issuing bank establishes its own policies regarding interest rates charged, grace periods, and other factors relating to the card. Annual membership fees may also be different at each issuing bank but they are generally lower than those of general-purpose cards. Usually, additional cards for family members are free.

Because there is so much competition among local and even regional banks for your credit card business, and because each bank sets its own fees, interest rates, credit approval standards, etc., it may pay you to keep abreast of what is currently being offered, even if you already have a card from one bank. Sometimes a bank eager to promote or expand its credit card business may offer such things as free membership for a year, or interest rates that are, for a while, a few percentage points below those of competitors. These are opportunities to save yourself some money. If you have a good credit record and, most important, the discipline to use your credit cards wisely, it may make sense to have credit cards from more than one bank, using the one with the lowest interest rate and/or longest grace period.

There is, however, the very real danger that having more than one credit card (and thus a bigger combined credit line to draw upon) will only multiply your risk of digging yourself into a deep financial hole. Unless you are absolutely certain you can keep things under control, don't have more than one active card of any type.

Bank credit cards usually have a predefined credit limit, perhaps as high as $5,000 to qualified individuals, based on a review of the application form and a credit report (higher limits are available on so-called "premium cards"). There is considerable overlap of various features among the different cards, so make sure you understand which one provides you the services you will use most.

Because of the local variations, all MasterCards are not the same; neither are all Visa cards. There may be a considerable difference between a Visa card and a MasterCard issued by the same bank, although at some banks they operate exactly the same way. You should investigate this potential difference very carefully, especially since many of the local bank's personnel are not familiar with all the aspects of their bank's credit card setup.

Make sure you get the information regarding interest rates, grace periods, methods of computing interest, etc. in writing. Do not depend on the bank's preprinted, credit card marketing brochures for accuracy, as they are worded as broadly and unspecifically as possible to last as long as possible before changes make them obsolete.

Here's one real life example of why all MasterCard and Visa cards should not necessarily be used the same way. Because of the policies set by the author's own bank for the MasterCards and Visa cards they issued at the time of this writing, each card had its own unique advantages and disadvantages, especially when it came to how much and when interest was charged. Depending on how the credit card holder intended to repay, the financial costs could be quite different.

In July 1989, for purchase charges made with this bank's MasterCard, a 25-day grace period (from the statement date) for payment was allowed before a finance charge at 18 percent APR (retroactive to the transaction recording date) was incurred. By comparison, their Visa card allowed no grace period, and interest, at $17^1/8$ percent (calculated at prime x 1.25 + 4 percent), was charged from the date the charge transaction was first recorded.

Given these facts, there was a case to be made for having both cards, using one or the other depending on when you planned to pay the charge balance. If you could pay the charge balance within the 25-day grace period, you would use the MasterCard, even though it potentially had the higher rate of interest (18 percent). If you suspected you might not be able to pay the charge balance when due, you would use the Visa card, which had a lower rate of interest ($17^{1}/_{8}$ percent).

Premium bank credit cards

It is confusing to generalize about differences between regular and so-called "premium" credit cards. Just as there are American Express Gold or Platinum cards with higher credit limits, extra privileges, and benefits, so are there banks that issue premium cards with added features. The names may vary from bank to bank—"Preferred," or "Gold," or any other such name to differentiate them from their "ordinary" counterparts. Such cards normally have a higher annual membership fee, although the Discover card, issued by Sears, has no annual fee and has some features of both regular and premium bank cards.

Premium cards generally offer a substantially higher credit limit, subject to request and a credit report. Some cards offer up to a 1 percent refund on aggregate purchases charged on the card during the year. That may not be as big a deal as you might think since you get back only $10 for every $1,000 you spend. After spending perhaps $50 or more in membership fees, you really have to use the card a great deal to get ahead. Of course, the credit card companies know quite well that the more you use the card, the more chance you will end up paying them interest when you can't keep the balance current.

CONVENIENCE AND CREDIT AT A PRICE

There is no question about it; credit cards are convenient. But that convenience can challenge the willpower of even the most frugal of people. Other than gambling, you would be hard pressed to find a more frequent method of self-inflicted financial disaster than through the use and abuse of credit cards. Given the relative ease in obtaining credit cards, and the fact that they may permit you more total credit than you are financially capable of handling, you should avoid having them at all until you and others in your family consistently demonstrate the ability to live within a budget. If you cannot do that, don't get any. Or destroy the cards and pay off what you owe.

GUARANTEED CREDIT CARDS

Some organizations advertise their ability to get you a credit card if you are unable to obtain a bank credit card on your own because of a poor credit history. Usually they get the card by having you make a deposit that is held as full security by the issuing bank for any and all charges made against the credit card. The credit card will have a credit limit equal to or less than the amount of funds on deposit as security.

CHAPTER VIII

Protecting yourself

M any banks will offer to reduce their interest rate charge to you by ¹/₄ percent or so if you agree to permit your monthly loan payments to be automatically charged against your checking or savings account with them. They will stress the convenience (you don't have to remember to write a check each month) and the money you can save in interest.

CUTTING THE INTEREST?

At a ¹/₄ percent reduction, you save $2.50 per thousand dollars of principal per year—not much of a savings. And the checking and/or savings account balances you have retained at the bank to allow the automatic transfer will be vulnerable to seizure through the "set-off" provisions that are probably included in the loan agreement. In the event you run into trouble making payments on your loan, the minor interest savings might turn out to be a very expensive option.

WHO SIGNS?

A husband and wife almost always assume that both must sign any and all loan or credit agreements. Lenders are perfectly happy to let you think so because it's to their advantage. But legally, there is not such a requirement. In fact, it is not in your best interest for both of you to sign, and it should be avoided if at all possible.

If the loan is to be secured by collateral and that collateral is owned in part by husband and wife, the lending organization will correctly insist that both spouses sign the loan agreement. However, a loan not collateralized by jointly owned property does not legally require the signature of anyone other than the person upon whose creditworthiness and/or income the loan has been granted. While laws vary from state to state (especially so-called "community property" laws), you should check this out before both spouses automatically sign any loan document.

In the event of a loan default, if only one spouse has signed, the creditor has much less flexibility in who can be pursued during its debt collection efforts. There is no need to subject all of the family's assets or earnings to seizure and attachment if it isn't necessary.

I DIDN'T SIGN THAT!

Never, never sign a blank agreement! Under no circumstances should you ever sign any agreement, contract, or other document if all the agreed upon terms and conditions have not been filled in first. No matter what you are promised verbally, no matter how inconvenient it may be, always insist that everything be put in writing before you sign. If there are blank spaces in the documents that do not require information, draw a line or put "X's" in those spaces so that nothing can be inserted there after you sign. You must also read the contract completely before you sign. If you do not understand something, don't be embarrassed; ask for a complete explanation. Always get a copy of what you have signed before you leave; don't wait for it to be mailed to you.

COOLING-OFF PERIOD

Anytime an agreement requires you to put up your home as collateral, the laws in most states (under certain conditions and limitations) grant you three days to think it over before the

Real life, real answers.

After living in their home for almost 40 years, the Cranes decided to have new, energy-saving siding put on all the outside walls when they saw an advertisement that promised "Five-year terms—12 percent financing to qualified buyers."

The salesman presented them with a quote of $5,000 for the job and promised they would save enough money in heating and cooling expenses to recover their investment in five years. He filled out a combination purchase/installment loan contract with the $5,000 price, but left the financing terms blank. He told the Cranes, "When your credit application is approved by the bank, I'll countersign the contract and return it to you."

The Cranes signed the blank contract. They were given a copy of the quote, but they did not get a copy of the purchase/installment agreement or a right of rescission form. A week after the job was completed, the Cranes received a copy of the now filled-in contract, along with a payment book.

They were being charged at the rate of 16 percent interest with 36 monthly payments of $175.79 to be made over the next three years instead of the 12 percent, five-year contract at $111.22 per month they had expected.

"The bank wouldn't approve a five-year contract for a couple your age, and the interest rate is higher because of that," the salesman responded when the Cranes called to complain. To their dismay, they also found out that the contract contained terms that called for a lien to be placed against their house if they failed to make the payments called for.

Fortunately, they happened to tell their story at the next meeting of their Senior Citizens' Support Group chapter when a local TV reporter was present. He helped them get the bank to replace the installment contract with one that agreed with the original terms promised. When the local district attorney began an investigation of the siding contractor, the company was no longer in the area.

agreement becomes effective—a so-called cooling-off period. This "right of rescission" enables you to cancel the transaction if you so notify the seller in writing within the defined period. The seller must give you a correctly dated, special form in duplicate that explains your rights, one copy of which you must promptly mail back if you wish to cancel the contract. Make sure you act promptly; if more than three days have passed from the date of the agreement, you will probably be stuck with the contract.

A similar three-day cooling-off law exists regarding purchase agreements made with door-to-door salesmen. If the seller fails to give you a right of rescission form, you may have a longer period of time to cancel, but you will have to prove you were not given this form, which might be quite difficult. If you wish to cancel the deal, always mail the form back using certified or registered mail and retaining a copy within the time period allowed. If you intend to or have sent in your cancellation of the deal, don't let anyone (contractors, repairmen, deliverymen, etc.) make deliveries or start work; you might thereby revalidate the contract and/or incur liabilities.

FRAUDULENT DEBT MANAGEMENT SERVICES

Some underhanded organizations advertise their services as "debt managers," promising that, as experts, they will handle your finances and arrange to negotiate and prorate payments among your creditors. They will provide this service for a percentage of your paycheck. Unfortunately, a significant number of these organizations do not deliver what they promise. They charge you a hefty fee nonetheless, and you probably end up in even worse financial shape and with even angrier creditors.

If you do need help in a debt management program, use one of the nationally recognized, nonprofit, consumer credit counseling services advertised in the "Human Services" section of your local phone book. If you have any doubts regarding the integrity of any debt management service organization, check it out with the local Better Business Bureau, or the consumer protection department of your state attorney general's office.

"RULE OF 78s"

The credit industry has a fairly standard practice of penalizing anyone attempting to pay off a loan before it is due. The Federal Truth in Lending Act requires that the loan contract state clearly what, if any, penalties might be assessed in the event of prepayment. Sometimes there is clause in the agreement in which a prepayment penalty is stated in dollars. In other situations, there may be a reference to the "rule of 78s," an adaptation of a mathematical technique called "the sum of the integers."

The effect of the "rule of 78s" is to load more of the interest payments into the early part of the loan term and less into the later part. Thus, the first month's interest is 12/78s of the interest for the year; the second month's is 11/78s; the third month's is 10/78s; and so on, with the twelfth month's being 1/78s. Adding up all those fractional 78s gives you 78/78s, or 100 percent of the interest for the year.

If you pay back a loan after three months, instead of being charged only 25 percent of the year's interest (for the one-quarter of the year you had the loan), you will pay 42.3 percent of the year's interest under the "rule of 78s" (12/78s + 11/78s + 10/78s = 33/78s = 42.3 percent).

Assume a $5,000, one-year loan at 13 percent APR for a total annual interest of $650 ($5,000 x 13 percent). If you decided to repay early, say at the end of three months, you would think you would have to pay the total of $5,000 in principal plus $162.50 in interest (representing one-fourth of the $650 interest charge for the full year), for a total of $5,162.50 in principal and interest.

Not so! The lender would say, "We are entitled to the first three months' interest according to the 'rule of 78s'—that is 33/

78s or 42.3 percent of the $650 in interest for the year, equaling $275. If you wish to repay, give us $5,275 ($5,000 + $275)."

Thus, even though you held the loan for only 25 percent of the time you contracted for (three months out of twelve months or 3/12s = 25 percent), you will pay 42.3 percent of the total interest for twelve months. It may not sound fair, but it is perfectly legal.

Some loan agreements will state they use the actuarial method for computing interest due on prepayments. This method is fair to you. Under the actuarial method, you are charged $1/12$ of the interest for each month the loan has been outstanding.

Whether or not you think you may want to prepay a loan, always ask the lender to spell out exactly what the terms and conditions of prepayment would be.

CREDIT INSURANCE

Almost all credit-granting organizations (banks, credit card companies, department stores, finance companies, etc.) will attempt to include, at additional cost, credit life, disability, and/ or health and accident insurance coverage in connection with the debt contract.

Generally speaking, there is no legal requirement that you purchase such insurance. You should not permit yourself to be forced or frightened into signing up for it unless, after examining all the pros and cons, you decide to take it. Most experts agree that purchasing the insurance packages offered by the credit-granting organizations may not be necessary, and that they are much more costly than other insurance available from your own insurance agent.

Frequently, when offered to you by a credit card company or in connection with a department store charge account, the insurance premium cost may be quoted to you as " $x per $100 of the average daily balance of your loan balance." In an auto or other installment loan, it might be expressed as, "Your monthly payment for the loan without insurance is $211.71, and only $216.63 with credit life insurance."

These insurance policies are a form of decreasing term insurance, with the amount of the insurance coverage decreasing as the loan balance is reduced. Thus, if you have a $10,000, four-year auto installment loan, every time you make a monthly loan payment, the insurance coverage goes down accordingly, decreasing to zero when the last monthly payment is made and the loan is finally paid off. The insurance premium, however, does not decrease because it is set up to be a fixed portion of every monthly payment. In fact, the way it usually works is that the insurance premium for the entire loan term is added to the loan up front; and you are borrowing the premium (and paying interest on it) just as if it were another car equipment option. Here's a typical example of the monthly payments on a $10,000 auto loan at 12 percent APR for 48 months, with and without additional insurance coverage:

Description	Monthly Payment	Total of 48 Payments
No insurance coverage	$264.64	$12,702.72
With life insurance coverage	$270.79	$12,997.92
With accident and health coverage	$276.77	$13,284.96
With life and accident/health coverage	$283.51	$13,608.48

Over the four-year term of the loan, you would be paying a total of $295.20 for the life insurance ($233.54 premium + $61.66 interest); $582.24 for the accident and health coverage ($460.62 premium + $121.62 interest); and $905.76 ($716.57 premium + $189.19 interest) for a package of life insurance plus accident and health insurance.

If insurance coverage is purchased, the loan balance at any point in time will be paid off in the event an insured party suffers a covered catastrophe (death, disability, etc.). Should you have such insurance coverage? If so, should you purchase it from the creditor?

If you purchase the insurance and the worst happens, the check for the insurance proceeds goes to the creditor, not to your family. Therefore, the primary beneficiary of the insurance is the creditor, not your family. Perhaps it would be better for your family to continue to make the monthly loan payments instead of having the creditor get paid off at once through the insurance (and getting more profit on a prepayment through the rule of 78s described above). Maybe the money you were paying to insure that *the creditor* got paid could have gone for some other, more important family purpose or need.

So-called credit life insurance offered with loan packages is almost always considerably more expensive than similar, or better, term insurance from an independent insurance agent. If, however, you have a medical condition that might preclude you from purchasing term insurance on your own, the plans in connection with installment loans and other credit may be the only way to acquire insurance.

The disability insurance coverage offered with loans may be, in part, the most cost-effective way of obtaining such coverage. It may be difficult to find alternative coverage at an equal or better premium cost because there are fewer insurance companies offering disability insurance policies to individuals. You should check the existence and adequacy of your present coverage. It may be cheaper to purchase equal or better disability insurance as an additional rider or option to the personal insurance you already own.

You will seldom have the chance to review the various terms and conditions of an insurance policy sold by a credit-granting organization before you are asked to sign it. In fact, the policy may not be sent to you until weeks afterward. The wisest course is to discuss your insurance needs with your own insurance agent before you take out a loan. Don't rely on an auto salesman, department store credit clerk, or bank clerk to give you sound insurance advice.

CHAPTER IX

Trouble

T he slide into a personal financial crisis can have many different causes—losing your job; a layoff, strike, or illness; uninsured medical bills; uninsured casualty losses; divorce; a death in the family; or another sudden event. A bit slower but just as disastrous are the effects of overspending; relying on debt to enjoy a higher lifestyle; neglecting to pay bills and debts promptly; failing to save up an emergency cash reserve; gambling; or counting on some windfall or future event to bail you out.

IN OVER YOUR HEAD

While you can purchase insurance to protect yourself and your family against the financial pressure caused by some unfortunate events, such as death or disability, you remain vulnerable to others. A large proportion of the individuals and families who find themselves in severe financial difficulties are victims of their own behavior. Most of these people ignored the early-warning signs of a disaster in the making—signs that appeared at a time when it would have been easier and less traumatic to straighten things out.

PREVENTION IS EASIER THAN THE CURE

The earliest symptom of all is the complete absence of any form of money management plan. If you don't have some sort of budget that keeps track of how much money you have available to spend and what you spend it on, you are a prime candidate for some sort of future financial trouble. This doesn't mean you need a sophisticated accounting system. Even putting money aside into a sugar bowl each week for certain expenses can be part of an intelligent and workable system.

The simple but comprehensive financial worksheets in Chapter II can serve as the basis for effective management of your finances. For more detailed help, you might turn to *The easy family budget*, another book in the *Real life, real answers* series. Remember that prevention is a family affair, not just the role of one of the spouses or the parents. Every family member old enough to spend money must be part of the program.

SYMPTOMS

If you agree with any of the following statements, you may be heading for some serious problems. The sooner you can get to their root causes, the easier they will be to eliminate.

1. You are not able to accumulate any money in a savings account.
2. You (and your spouse, if any) have no idea how much credit card spending you are doing until the monthly statement arrives.
3. You frequently have to borrow cash to meet your regular household expenses.
4. You regularly let some past due bills slide in order to pay other past due bills.
5. You are spending over 25 percent of your take-home income to pay installment bills or over 36 percent when mortgage payments are included.
6. You are getting dunning letters and phone calls from creditors.
7. You (and your spouse, if any) are always worried about meeting your bills and debts and arguing about spending money.

Facing reality is difficult, but looking at things squarely and honestly is absolutely necessary. Don't wait to do something about it. Delay can spell disaster. Getting out of trouble isn't nearly as easy as getting into trouble.

FIRST THINGS FIRST

Admittedly, being in financial difficulty is embarrassing, scary, and uncomfortable. But the worst thing you can do is attempt to duck or hide from your creditors. The second worst thing is to deal with them when you are unprepared. You cannot start repairing your situation unless you have a total and complete understanding of it. To deal intelligently with any one of your creditors, much less all of them, you must develop an accurate picture of your income, assets, and liabilities. Get all your unpaid bills together, the installment contracts, credit card statements, loan agreements—any and all documents pertaining to existing debt and financial commitments. Read those documents. If you don't understand them, have a knowledgeable and trusted friend or financial adviser explain them to you.

Get your paycheck stubs, last year's tax returns, and W-2 statements. Prepare the budget and net worth statements in Chapter II. Only when you know what and where the problems are, and what cash flow and assets you have to work with, can you then confront each situation with the best chance of resolving it in a satisfactory manner.

If you don't deal with your predicament promptly, the problems will get worse. The pressure will mount, the demands will escalate, and creditors will grow less cooperative or patient.

YOU DO HAVE RIGHTS

Sometimes the collection pressure from your creditors may take illegal forms. Why? Because creditors have found it effective to embarrass and panic people unable to pay their debts on time. The more they pressure you, the more likely you will pay them and not some other creditor.

The federal Fair Debt Collection Practices Act (and possibly some laws in your state) gives you protection from many of the illegal practices employed by some creditors, their collection agencies, and their lawyers. Among other things, creditors and their agents are not permitted to abuse or harass you; call you at an unusual time or place (including at work, if you object); or employ false or misleading threats, representations, or unfair practices. Failure to observe the provisions of the law subjects the creditor to severe financial fines and penalties if you register a complaint and are upheld.

There are a number of federal, state, and local agencies that will help you. Included among these are the Federal Trade Commission; the consumer relations department of the nearest Federal Reserve Bank; the Department of Justice; the attorney general's office; your congressman; your state's attorney general, Justice Department, or Department of Consumer Affairs; and a number of local, nonprofit consumer affairs agencies. The federal government has a local phone number to the Federal Information Center, and many states have a governor's hot line phone number to provide assistance to citizens with problems and complaints. All of the numbers are in your local phone book.

Familiarize yourself with your rights under the law. You can obtain pamphlets describing most federal laws pertaining to consumers' rights relating to credit from any regional office of the Federal Trade Commission, or by calling their main office in Washington, DC, at (202) 326-2000. Even if you are not familiar with the laws, if what is being done to you seems wrong or unfair, do not hesitate to contact one or more of the agencies listed above.

If you believe you are being illegally harassed and abused by a creditor, collection agency, or attorney, the first step is to contact the highest official in the creditor's organization you can reach by phone. Coolly and calmly tell that person of the abuse that is taking place, and that you are registering a formal complaint in accordance with the provisions of the Fair Debt Collection Practices Act. Immediately follow up with a letter to that official, sent by certified mail, describing your complaint and confirming the phone conversation. If the illegal harassment continues, contact the nearest office of the Consumer Protection Bureau of the Federal Trade Commission as well as any appropriate local or state government or consumer agencies.

If you dispute the debt or don't believe you owe as much as the creditor claims, by all means let the creditor, collection agent, or lawyer know that—in writing. Were the goods you are being billed for received? Were they damaged? Ask for verification and proof of the debt and how it is being calculated.

Under the federal Fair Credit Billing Act, you have the right to dispute an error in billing, and the creditor must acknowledge and investigate your complaint. While that investigation is proceeding, you cannot be forced to pay the disputed amount.

When dealing with creditors, always keep a record of when (date and time) you contacted or tried to contact them, when they contacted you, to whom you spoke (name and title), and what was said, promised, or agreed. You should *always* confirm all verbal agreements in writing; don't wait for the creditor to do it. Never give up an original copy of any financial document unless you have a duplicate or legible photocopy.

You will find that your creditors will treat you with greater respect if they know that you know your rights.

DEBT CONSOLIDATION

Generally, the solution to a financial crisis caused by overuse of credit lies in reducing your rate of expenditures to the absolute minimum in order to provide the cash flow to pay off the creditors over time. You may also have to liquidate some assets and use the proceeds to pay debt. The creation of any new debt must be avoided unless it is part of a logical debt consolidation and restructuring program.

A debt consolidation loan may allow you to reduce the aggregate monthly payments you are required to make on existing debt by giving you more time to pay off your total debt. Using the proceeds of the debt consolidation loan, you pay off all the other existing debt and refrain from creating any new or additional debt. For example, assume you have the following debts and past due bills:

	Monthly Payment	Total Owed	Status
Installment loan	$250	$5,000	2 months late
Department store charge	50	850	3 months late
Bank overdraft loan	100	1,000	Current
Credit card A		500	2 months late
Credit card B		750	1 month late
Personal loan	500	4,000	2 months late
Totals	$900	$12,100	

Not counting the $1,250 now past due on your credit cards, you have to make $900 a month in payments for the foreseeable future. You have been unable to keep up with those payments and have fallen behind. The creditors are sending you dunning notices. A review of your income and budget indicates that if you maintain tight financial control over all of your expenditures, you can definitely manage $450 a month for debt payments. Before your credit rating is ruined by getting further behind, you should arrange a debt consolidation loan based upon your ability to make $450 in monthly payments.

You borrow the $12,100 required to pay everyone else off from either your bank or credit union. If the interest rate is, say 15 percent, you can get the $12,100 through a 33-month loan with a $450 monthly repayment. (Note that the bank or credit union might insist that the proceeds of the debt consolidation loan be disbursed directly to your creditors rather than turned over to you.) Through the debt consolidation loan, you have paid everyone else off and brought your bills up to date.

Your aggregate monthly payments have been reduced from $900 to a more manageable $450, although you will now be paying back a total of $14,850 (33 x $450). You must now make sure that you live within your budget, keep current on your new loan, and not fall back into the bad spending and credit habits that got you into trouble. While a debt consolidation loan is an expensive way to work through a financial crisis, if you have a steady income it is an effective option.

REPAYMENT PLANS

While creditors may tell you they are not interested in your personal problems and only want to get paid, that is not necessarily the whole truth. If you tell them how you got into trouble (it usually doesn't pay to lie about this) and what your plans are for getting yourself out of it, you show them you are not a deadbeat, but just an average person who has had a very common problem. Most reputable businesses will go along with you if both you and your repayment plan are reasonable. After all, they probably don't want back the merchandise they sold you, and collection agencies and legal actions are both expensive and time-consuming. If you can make payments, albeit smaller ones, they still will be collecting principal and interest.

If you approach your creditors with a comprehensive plan to work things out, usually offering smaller payments and stretching out the payment terms, chances are you will be successful. Obviously, the plan must be logical and reasonable. You cannot expect any creditor to accept a plan that indicates you won't be making any payments during the month of July because you will be spending two weeks on a vacation trip to the Rocky Mountains.

Your plan must clearly demonstrate the changes or sacrifices you and your family intend to make in order to free up additional cash to pay your creditors. You might have to sell the Volvo Turbo sedan and replace it with a cheaper Ford Escort. Maybe the kids' dancing lessons will have to wait for better times. No creditor is likely to accept any plan that indicates you intend to maintain exactly the same lifestyle as before while he or she waits for the money.

Real life, real answers.

A lthough both of them were earning good money, Paul and Kate Brown's accumulated debt had become so large that they were unable to keep current with the payments. After reviewing their situation with an attorney, they decided to work out payment extensions with their creditors. They prepared a strict budget and financial plan. Each creditor accepted the payout plan and agreed in writing to cease collection and dunning efforts.

One of the largest creditors (a local department store) was using an overly zealous collection agency that did not stop its collection attempts. In fact, the agency began using some illegal tactics. They called the Browns' home at all hours of the night. When the Browns called the department store to complain, the credit manager blamed a mix-up in communications and promised the matter would be taken care of immediately.

In spite of reassurances given the Browns over the next two weeks, the harassment continued. The collection agency threatened the Browns with seizure of their car and made three embarrassing calls to the personnel department of Paul's employer.

The Browns made a personal visit to the credit manager. They took copies of all pertinent correspondence, including a record of the calls made by the agency to their home and Paul's employer. They advised the store of their intention to file a formal complaint with the Federal Trade Commission under the Fair Debt Collection Practices Act.

Faced with incontrovertible evidence of the harassment caused by *their* agent, the credit manager realized the potential liability his company faced. He immediately called the president of the collection agency and terminated its involvement with the Browns as well as its relationship with the store. He also offered to waive all interest due on the money owed if the Browns would continue to make the payments as promised and not file a complaint.

More than likely, each creditor will insist on getting a bigger payment than you have offered, but you must resist the pressure. If you show your creditors your total plan, indicating the need to make some payments to each of them, you will demonstrate a balanced plan that is not subject to much tinkering by any one creditor. The key is to stay in control of the situation, to make sure *you* decide who gets what and when.

Once having gotten the creditors to agree to your plan, you *absolutely, unconditionally* must live up to it. Whatever new promises and commitments you have given them must be honored. Nothing gets a creditor angrier than discovering that, once having given a debtor some slack and extra time, the debtor then fails to live up to the new agreement. The creditor will lose his or her patience and willingness to cooperate.

For this reason, you must make certain that the commitments you make as part of your plan are reasonable under the normal anticipated circumstances. The plan must not depend on some miraculous event or intricate combination of several things happening at the right time and place. If there are parts of your plan that are dependent on specific things happening, then disclose those things to the creditors up front. Let them judge in advance the likelihood of these events occurring. Once you have done that, they have implicitly accepted the contingent nature of parts of the plan and are less likely to have an extreme reaction if something is delayed. When you have their agreement, confirm it in writing.

No matter how well thought out the plan, something may happen to make it impossible for you to honor your new commitments. Again, let the creditors know *immediately*—as far in advance of your next payment date as possible. If you can offer an alternate date or plan that makes sense, do so. Obviously, they are not going to be pleased, so you have to expect some unpleasantness. One thing you must not do is let the payment date pass in silence and hope the creditors forget about it.

CREDIT COUNSELING SERVICES

Most cities have organizations or agencies (for example, Consumer Credit Counseling Service, or Family Service Agency) that provide credit counseling services and advice to individuals and families. These services are provided at no charge or at a nominal cost. If you need help with preparing your budget, or are already in financial trouble and need assistance in developing a plan for dealing with creditors, you should contact one of these counseling organizations. They are usually listed in the "Human Services" section of your local phone directory. You can also contact the National Foundation for Consumer Credit, Inc. (8701 Georgia Avenue, Suite 507, Silver Spring, MD 20910); phone (301) 589-5600.

THE FINE PRINT

Federal, state, and local laws grant certain legal rights in the event you fall behind in making your payments and/or default on your debt (fail to repay). In addition, charge account and credit card applications, loan agreements, and mortgage documents may contain clauses giving the creditor certain additional legal rights because you agree to waive rights and protection you, the debtor, would otherwise have under the law. Always read the documents you are being asked to sign. Frequently, these clauses (sometimes referred to as boilerplate information or the fine print) are on the reverse side of the documents you sign, but there is usually a sentence somewhere on the front that states that the terms and conditions on the reverse side are part of the contract or agreement.

It is difficult for the average person to understand what these clauses mean. They are carefully worded in precise legal language. Take your time and read them. The creditor's representative may tell you impatiently that they are only standard terms and not to be worried about. But don't allow yourself to be rushed. Just because terms have been preprinted on a form doesn't necessarily make them acceptable. If you don't understand the clause, ask that it be clearly explained to you. Better yet, have it explained to you by someone you know and in whom you have confidence.

LEGAL ACTION

If satisfactory arrangements have not been made with creditors, they may start legal action against you. You will be sent an official summons advising you that you are being sued by the creditor and giving a date, time, and place for a court appearance. You usually aren't given much notice—maybe a month, usually a lot less.

You should not ignore the summons. If you fail to appear at court, you will automatically lose, and the creditor will win by default. Get yourself a lawyer if you can afford one. If you cannot afford one or don't know one, call the local Consumer Credit Counseling Service or the local Legal Aid Society for assistance.

During the time between the receipt of the summons and the court date, it is still possible for you to work out some sort of agreement with the creditor and avoid the court appearance. Many creditors will insist that you communicate with their lawyers to work things out, but you should attempt to contact both the creditors and their lawyers.

If you reach a pay-off or stretch-out agreement, the summons can be canceled. Get that agreement in writing, and make sure the summons has been withdrawn or dismissed by the creditor's attorney (contact the administrative officer of the court to be sure). If you are not certain the summons has been withdrawn as promised, go to court on the day and time specified, bringing along all the documents pertaining to the debt, including a copy of the pay-off or stretch-out agreement.

Sometimes the court summons is never received by the debtor. While it is illegal, it is not unusual for some unscrupulous lawyers or process servers to deliberately fail to have the summons delivered. Since you don't know about the court date, you don't appear and thus, automatically, lose. Another dirty trick is to sue you in a court located so far from your home that it is impossible for you to get there. If either one of these two things happens to you, call one of the nonprofit consumer assistance or legal aid agencies immediately.

POWERFUL REMEDIES

The contract terms of installment loans and other loans and mortgages secured by collateral have clauses that give the creditor the right to repossess or seize the property described in the contract. Also, if you have lost your case in court, the creditor may be awarded a judgment lien against any of your assets; these can then be seized for resale by the creditor. The creditor also adds legal costs, repossession expenses, and additional interest to the original debt balance. When a creditor seizes the property, you have lost the ability to control when, where, and for how much the property will be sold. The creditor is supposed to sell the property for a fair price in a reasonable manner, but don't count on it. If the sale doesn't yield enough to pay off the total amount you owe, you are still liable for the balance.

Most bank loan agreements include a clause that gives the bank the right of "set-off." If you have a loan at a bank where you maintain savings and checking accounts and you are overdue in your loan payments, the set-off clause gives the bank the right to seize the money in those accounts—often with no notice—to apply against your debt. This can occur even if those accounts were not pledged as collateral or security for the loan. If you do get a loan from a bank, it may be prudent to limit the balance of funds accumulating in that bank in order to minimize the effects of a set-off action.

Garnishment is a legal process authorized by the court

wherein your employer is ordered to turn over a portion of each and every one of your paychecks directly to the creditor until your debt is paid off. There are federal and state laws limiting the amount or percentage of your wages that may be garnisheed, but it is a very effective collection process. Garnishment may have a negative influence on how you are viewed by your employer. Once your wages are garnisheed, not only do you have no control over where a significant portion will go, but you will have less to live on.

Many installment and other loan agreements contain a confession of judgment clause under which the debtor waives certain important legal rights he or she might otherwise have had under the law. While not legal or enforceable in all states, when and where the clause is legal the creditor has the authority to take immediate action to seize and sell property belonging to the debtor if the debtor misses so much as one payment. If at all possible, have this clause stricken from any agreement before you sign it. Precisely because of the power it gives the creditor, this may be difficult to accomplish.

CHAPTER X

Bankruptcy

V oluntary personal bankruptcy is a complex legal process whereby a debtor formally acknowledges to a court that he or she cannot pay his or her debts. That person petitions the court for its protection while a plan of action to liquidate the debtor's assets to pay off and/or otherwise discharge the claims of the various creditors is accomplished.

Bankruptcy is neither a quick fix nor a Band-Aid; it is serious medicine. A bankruptcy can remain on your credit record for up to 10 years, after which, by law, it must be removed. During that period, your ability to obtain credit will be seriously impaired.

A WAY OUT?

Does the fact that there is a growing number of individuals filing for voluntary bankruptcy indicate that bankruptcy is a good thing for the typical, hard-pressed borrower? Not really. Bankruptcy carries with it an enormous financial and emotional penalty, but, under certain circumstances, it may be the lesser of two evils for someone hopelessly trapped under the credit grindstone. Deciding to file a petition for bankruptcy is not a step to be taken lightly or without serious investigation. Although there are a number of do-it-yourself kits on the market today, complete with standard forms and worksheets, you should get professional legal advice or the advice of a nonprofit consumer credit advisory agency.

Seeing themselves falling deeper and deeper into debt and anticipating bankruptcy, debtors sometimes try to transfer, give away, or hide assets so as not to lose them in the bankruptcy proceedings. Such actions may be illegal and fraudulent. If these actions took place within certain time limits before the bankruptcy was filed, the court may, on its own or upon petition of the creditors, set aside such transfers and recover the property. Courts do not look with favor on such tactics.

CHAPTER 7

Under this form of bankruptcy (named after a particular section of the federal bankruptcy laws), the debtor files a petition with the court listing all assets and liabilities. The petition also includes a listing of property claimed as being exempt from bankruptcy under federal and state law. Within specified dollar limits, certain assets (such as a limited amount of equity in a home, cars or personal property, some personal jewelry, professional tools or equipment needed to earn a living, Social Security payments, veterans and pension benefits, etc.) are classified as exempt, and may not be taken from you when you file bankruptcy.

The court then holds a meeting with you and your creditors, all of whom will have been notified directly and/or through public notice. The court appoints a trustee who then takes control of all your assets for purposes of liquidating those not deemed exempt. The proceeds are used to pay off your creditors to the extent possible. Note that some of the nonexempt assets may temporarily remain in your possession during the liquidation process, but you are not permitted to sell, trade, lose, give away, destroy, return, or otherwise dispose of any such assets.

Once you have filed for bankruptcy, creditors must cease all collection efforts against you, although a creditor is permitted to continue collection efforts against any co-maker, co-signer, or guarantor of your debt. Creditors also have the right to contest actions and decisions of the trustee, in which case the bankruptcy judge will render the final decision.

Ultimately, when the trustee completes the liquidation and disbursement of proceeds, a Notice of Discharge is issued to you. This document prevents your creditors from henceforth collecting the debts listed in the bankruptcy proceedings, even if there were insufficient proceeds from the asset liquidation to pay them off in whole or in part.

There are some debts and obligations that cannot be discharged in a Chapter 7 bankruptcy proceeding, including, but not limited to, alimony and child support, real estate or personal property used as security or collateral for a loan, and debts resulting from misrepresentation, fraud, or other illegal acts on your part.

CHAPTER 13

If the amount of your secured and unsecured debts is below specified dollar limits, and you have a regular income that can reasonably be expected to continue, you can file a Chapter 13 bankruptcy petition. This type of bankruptcy is often referred to as "the wage-earner plan."

Under this type of bankruptcy, you submit a plan, through the court, to your creditors. In this plan you offer to repay all or some of your debts (say 60 cents, 30 cents, or less on each dollar owed) over a specified period of time (not to exceed five years), based on anticipated income. All creditors are offered the same terms or percentage payoff. The court will decide whether the plan is fair and reasonable. Your creditors vote to accept or reject the plan.

The fact that it is possible for you to refile under a Chapter 7 bankruptcy if the creditors reject your Chapter 13 proposal serves as a powerful incentive for them to approve your offer. Once they do, a trustee is appointed to whom you must send the required payment amounts on schedule. Interest on the past debts ceases to accrue. While you are making the repayments, your creditors cannot evict you, repossess property, or file suit for past debts. You can, however, be sued for new debts incurred after the bankruptcy filing.

When you have made all the payments as per the plan (or been otherwise excused, under certain circumstances, by the court from making further payments), the court will grant you a discharge from bankruptcy. You will not be relieved of responsibility for alimony or child support.

During the time you are making the payments, the distribution of your income is under the control of the court, and you will live under tight budget restraints. If you get a raise, the trustee might allocate some or all of that raise to the payment plan.

Under Chapter 13, certain assets are exempt, as they are in a Chapter 7 bankruptcy. Your other nonexempt assets are not turned over to the trustee for sale; instead you are still able to retain and use them, including those that might have been given as collateral to secured creditors. All creditors' collection efforts must cease, including those against any co-signers or co-makers of your loans, unless and until you fail to complete your payoff plan.

During a bankruptcy proceeding, you may be approached by a creditor to "reaffirm" a specific debt. What you are being asked to do is to acknowledge that debt as being correct, and further, that you are willing to pay it irrespective of the bankruptcy proceedings. Reaffirmation of a debt is rarely in your best interests. In fact, the law has placed strict limits on your ability to reaffirm debt and has established preconditions and cancellation procedures for debtors who have unwisely given reaffirmation.

SHOULD YOU OR SHOULDN'T YOU?

Going bankrupt does not have the social stigma it once had, but it can be devastating to your future ability to get credit. A bankruptcy remains on your credit report for many years and scares off lenders. Basically, the decision to file for bankruptcy

Real life, real answers.

T wo years into their marriage, financial disaster struck Ralph and Betty Forte. Ralph's union went on a wildcat strike after a labor dispute that had already lasted over five months. Despite a few odd jobs doing house painting and Betty's meager earnings as a part-time waitress, the young couple were unable to earn enough to meet their existing financial commitments.

They still owed several thousand dollars for a two-week vacation cruise they had charged on their credit cards. Ralph had made only four installment payments on their new, giant-screen TV before the strike started. He also had two more years of car payments. When Ralph went out on strike, his employer automatically stopped making payments on his medical insurance coverage, and it became Ralph's responsibility to meet the $355 a month premium to continue the coverage. The few thousand dollars they had been saving for a down payment on their dream house had long since been spent paying normal day-to-day living expenses. Besides some furniture, clothing, an old car, and Betty's diamond engagement ring, the Fortes had little in the way of unencumbered assets.

The Fortes decided that their existing debts, financial obligations, and interest costs were hopelessly beyond their ability to pay as long as the strike continued. They talked to a lawyer and first considered a Chapter 13 bankruptcy. That would protect whatever assets they had, but without the prospects of a steady and stable income, they would be unable to submit a workable plan to the court.

They decided instead on a Chapter 7 bankruptcy. A record of the bankruptcy would go on their credit history and make it difficult, but not impossible, to obtain credit in the future. But they would eliminate the pressure from creditors and unburden their relationship of the tension their financial situation had caused.

is a tradeoff. Should you continue to suffer the torment of collection agents, wage garnishment, and seizure of property? Or should you seek the protection of the court and lose most of your property (Chapter 7) or a significant portion of your income for years (Chapter 13)?

Choosing between a Chapter 7 and a Chapter 13 depends on a variety of factors, including the amount and nature of your debts, the ratio of secured to unsecured debts, the kind and amount of property you own, and your projected income stream— all of which you might not be trained to evaluate properly. Discuss the matter in detail with the other members of your family and any co-signers or co-makers of any of your debts. While you can file for bankruptcy yourself without the use of a lawyer (and many people have done so successfully), if you have a reasonable amount at risk, you should discuss it with a qualified attorney first.

When meeting with a lawyer, make certain you fully understand how much the lawyer's services will cost you, what those services will be, and how you are expected to pay for them. Lawyers usually will ask for an advance payment as well as a series of progress payments. Don't hesitate to get price quotes from more than one qualified lawyer before you decide whom to hire.

REHABILITATING YOUR CREDIT RATING

It is possible to rehabilitate your credit rating even after bankruptcy. Of course, once you have paid off or settled past claims and debts, getting new credit will be extremely difficult. Nevertheless, you should begin the process once you are certain you can meet new financial obligations. It will take time to rebuild creditor confidence, but it can be done by paying bills on time and limiting the amount of credit sought. Collateral or co-signers will probably be needed, at least for a while.

CHAPTER XI

Making it work

C redit is a valuable, perhaps indispensable tool. It can also be irresistible and overwhelming. Reading this book has been an important first step in understanding how it can work for you.

A few basics bear repeating:

- ☐ Budgeting and planning your expenditures is fundamental to sound financial management.

- ☐ Taking periodic measurement of your net worth is the best way to evaluate progress toward your financial goals.

- ☐ The process of getting approved for credit depends on how you are "scored" based upon your personal situation, past history, and financial strength.

- ☐ It is often easier initially to get credit approval from organizations that sell products (department stores, auto dealers, etc.) than from other sources.

- ☐ Once having received credit, how you meet your financial obligations is made part of your financial history, and that information is available to others. Your ability to obtain additional credit in the future depends on your creditworthiness as reflected in that ongoing record.

- ☐ It is possible to get more credit than your income and your financial strength can reasonably support. Therefore, maintaining self-discipline is vital to keeping your financial affairs in order.

- ☐ How, when, and on what balance an interest charge is calculated can be as important as the interest rate itself. At any given APR, the simple interest/single payment loan is the least expensive basis for calculating interest. Add-on interest rates, while appearing low, are actually among the most expensive.

- A loan that is secured by the pledge of collateral places the collateral under risk of seizure and sale if the loan is not paid. Because a home equity loan requires your equity in the home to be pledged as collateral, great care should be taken before such a loan is made.

- Shopping for the best terms and conditions on loans before borrowing money can save you a great deal of money. Similarly, because not all credit cards are the same, investigate before you choose and use.

- Credit cards are convenient tools, but they are one of the most expensive ways to borrow money. Before using a credit card, know when and how you intend to pay for a purchase—there may be cheaper alternatives.

- Where possible, avoid having both spouses sign for a loan, and never sign any blank financial document. Always get a copy of any and all financial agreements when you sign them. If there is anything in the document you do not understand, have someone competent whom you trust explain it before you sign.

- Know your rights. A variety of federal, state, and local laws are in effect to ensure fair access to credit, disclosure of pertinent data, and reasonable collection practices. However, you cannot be totally protected from your own foolishness, ignorance, or greed.

- Bankruptcy is not an easy cure-all. It is a complex legal step with far-reaching effects that must not be taken lightly. Legal advice is necessary to determine whether and which bankruptcy is best for your situation.

- If you get in over your head, deal with your debt problems promptly. There are nonprofit agencies available to help.

Finally, getting into trouble is much easier than getting out of it. But there's no reason to have any trouble with credit now that you know how to use and enjoy it wisely.

Real life, real answers.

The up-to-date library of personal financial information

How to make basic investment decisions
by Neal Ochsner

Planning for a financially secure retirement
by Jim Jenks and Brian Zevnik

How to borrow money and use credit
by Martin Weiss

How to pay for your child's college education
by Chuck Lawliss and Barry McCarty

Your will and estate planning
by Fred Tillman and Susan G. Parker

How to protect your family with insurance
by Virginia Applegarth

The easy family budget
by Jerald W. Mason

How to buy your first home
by Peter Jones

Planning for long-term health care
by Harold Evensky

Financial planning for the two-career family
by Candace E. Trunzo